KREGEL CLASSIC SERMONS SERIES

CLASSIC SERMONS ON THE MIRACLES OF JESUS

Compiled by

Warren W. Wiersbe

kregel
PUBLICATIONS

Grand Rapids, MI 49501

Classic Sermons on the Miracles of Jesus,
compiled by Warren W. Wiersbe.

Copyright © 1995 by Kregel Publications. All rights reserved. No part of this book may be reproduced, stored in a retrieval system, or transmitted in any form or by any means—electronic, mechanical, photocopy, recording, or otherwise—without written permission of the publisher, except for brief quotations in printed reviews.

Published by Kregel Publications, a division of Kregel, Inc., P.O. Box 2607, Grand Rapids, MI 49501. Kregel Publications provides trusted, biblical publications for Christian growth and service. Your comments and suggestions are valued.

Cover photo: Copyright © 1995 Kregel Inc.
Cover and Book Design: Alan G. Hartman

Library of Congress Cataloging-in-Publication Data

Classic sermons on the miracles of Jesus / compiled by Warren W. Wiersbe.
    p.   cm.— (Kregel classic sermons series)
    Includes index.
    1. Jesus Christ—Miracles—Sermons. 2. Sermons, English. 3. Sermons, American. I. Wiersbe, Warren W. II. Series: Kregel classic sermons series.
BT366.C57   1995 232.9'55—dc20   95-16508
                                       CIP

ISBN 0-8254-3999-X (pbk.)

2 3 4 5 Printing / Year 99

Printed in the United States of America

CONTENTS

LIST OF SCRIPTURE TEXTS

PREFACE

THE *KREGEL CLASSIC SERMONS SERIES* is an attempt to assemble and publish meaningful sermons from master preachers about significant themes.

These are *sermons*, not essays or chapters taken from books about themes. Not all of these sermons could be called "great," but all of them are *meaningful*. They apply the truths of the Bible to the needs of the human heart, which is something that all effective preaching must do.

While some are better known than others, all of the preachers whose sermons I have selected had important ministries and were highly respected in their day. The fact that a sermon is included in this volume does not mean that either the compiler or the publisher agrees with or endorses everything that the man did, preached, or wrote. The sermon is here because it has a valued contribution to make.

These are sermons about *significant* themes. The pulpit is no place to play with trivia. The preacher has thirty minutes in which to help mend broken hearts, change defeated lives, and save lost souls. He can never accomplish this demanding ministry by distributing homiletical tidbits. In these difficult days we do not need "clever" pulpiteers who discuss the times; we need dedicated ambassadors who will preach the eternities.

The reading of these sermons can enrich your spiritual life. The studying of them can enrich your skills as an interpreter and expounder of God's truth. However God uses these sermons in your life and ministry, my prayer is that His church around the world will be encouraged and strengthened by them.

WARREN W. WIERSBE

Empty Waterpots

J. Vernon McGee (1904–1988) is best remembered as the voice of "Through the Bible" radio broadcast, an international ministry that continues though Dr. McGee is now with the Lord. He pastored churches in Georgia, Texas, and California, most notably the Church of the Open Door in Los Angeles (1949–1970). He also taught at Biola (1943–1952). His practical verse-by-verse exposition of the Word of God, reminiscent of H. A. Ironside, endeared him to millions of believers who heard him in person and over the radio.

This message was given at the 1968 Founder's Week Conference of the Moody Bible Institute in Chicago and was originally published in *Founder's Week Messages—1968*. It is used by permission of the Moody Bible Institute.

J. Vernon McGee

1

EMPTY WATERPOTS

Jesus saith unto her, Woman, what have I to do with thee? Mine hour is not yet come. His mother saith unto the servants, Whatsoever he saith unto you, do it (John 2:5–5).

I'M SURE MOST of you recognize that the wedding at Cana has often been set before us as a picture of the wedding of Christ and the church someday, that He began His ministry by going to this wedding and He will conclude, as far as the church is concerned, with the marriage supper of the Lamb.

Then there are those who draw from this story a marvelous, wonderful, practical lesson, that our Lord is interested in marriages that are made down here. He began His ministry at this wedding in Cana instead of in Jerusalem, the religious center.

I think both these views are true. But I also think there is for us in this story another very practical and spiritual and wonderful lesson that I trust may be helpful as we begin this conference together, and it goes back to the request the mother of our Lord put to Him when this embarrassing thing took place—they ran out of wine.

Cana is not very far from Nazareth, and Mary had gone to the wedding ahead of Jesus and His disciples. I was rather surprised myself the first time I took a trip to the Holy Land to discover how close the two towns were. I ran out of film as we were leaving Nazareth, and by the time I could reload my camera, we were in Cana.

Mary was evidently a friend of those in the wedding party. And some think those in the home where the wedding took place may even have been relatives of Mary. At any rate Mary took a principal part in the preparation of the wedding feast, and our Lord and His disciples were invited.

The family was obviously of very meager means; they did not have enough refreshments to go around. Certainly I've never been to a wedding where they ran out of refreshments; that's something that just doesn't happen. But here these evidently poor folk experienced this embarrassing moment when they lacked wine. And for some unaccountable reason, the mother of Jesus (and she's never called Mary in the Gospel of John) said to Him, "They have no wine."

What did she mean by that? There have been several explanations. Some have said that it was just a gentle hint for Him and His disciples to depart, but I do not think that was it. John Calvin said she was suggesting that Jesus occupy the minds of the guests with a discourse. But I don't think that's really what Mary had in mind at all. I believe the context reveals what she had in mind, and that was that He perform a miracle. His answer, I think, indicates that. "Jesus saith unto her, Woman, what have I to do with thee? Mine hour is not yet come."

If I may paraphrase, what Mary said is simply this: "Here is Your opportunity to demonstrate that I have been right for thirty years—that You were virgin born and that You are the Son of God. This is an appropriate place and time, at a wedding, for You to perform a miracle that will make it clear of whom You are." I think that's what she had in mind. For thirty years she'd been under a cloud. From the day she said to the angel Gabriel, "Behold the handmaid of the Lord," she had moved under a cloud, and she and her son stayed under that cloud for thirty-three years.

One of the Messianic psalms (it's also an imprecatory psalm), Psalm 69, contains a strange statement which our Lord applied to Himself: "I am become a stranger unto my brethren, and an alien unto my mother's children. [Notice He did not say, "my father's children."] For the zeal of thine house hath eaten me up; and the reproaches of those who reproached thee are fallen upon me. When I wept, and chastened my soul with fasting, that was to my reproach. I made sackcloth also my garment; and I became a proverb to them" (vv. 8–11). I do not have to suggest to you tonight what that proverb was—what they called Him in Nazareth. Notice the next verse: "They that sit in the gate speak against me, and I was the song of the drunkards." The drunkards down at the corner saloon in Nazareth made up dirty little ditties about Jesus and His mother. He went through a cloud all those years.

Have you ever stopped to think that He suffered all this in order that you and I may have a clear title to heaven—that we may someday stand as legitimate sons of God in His presence and be able to say, "I know whom I have believed"—and that we may now have the authority to become the sons of God by trusting Christ.

Now Mary is saying to Him, "They have no wine. This is Your opportunity." And He answers her, "Woman, what have I to do with thee? Mine hour is not yet come." In other words, "This is not My time. This is not the time for Me to act." But move along three more years and He's hanging on the Cross and she's standing beneath. Now He looks down at her and says, "Woman, behold thy son!"— "My hour now has come. In three days I'll be back from the dead."

Paul says Jesus was "declared to be the Son of God with power, according to the spirit of holiness, by the resurrection from the dead" (Rom. 1:4). His resurrection didn't make Him the Son of God, but it declared who He was. And Mary's name was cleared.

Dr. Luke tells us that after our Lord ascended, Mary was in the upper room with the rest of the believers (Acts 1:13–14). And I am of the opinion that as she sat there with the others, she would say, "See, Thomas, didn't I tell you He was virgin born? Didn't I tell you, Simon Peter, that He was virgin born?"

At the wedding in Cana of Galilee He will perform no miracle to clear Mary's name. That's not the purpose of this miracle at all as we shall see. Notice, though, what He did. "His mother saith unto the servants, Whatever he saith unto you, do it." For thirty years I have wanted to preach a Mother's Day sermon on this verse: "His mother saith unto the servants, Whatever he saith unto you, do it." That was the best mother's advice I think I've ever heard of.

Now we come to what apparently was the most important part of the wedding, in verse 6: "There were set there six waterpots of stone, after the manner of the purifying of the Jews, containing two or three firkins apiece." These six waterpots were there for ceremonial cleansing according to the Levitical ritual. This was an elaborate ritual— there was constant washing going on, and through it God was teaching that those who come to Him for salvation must be clean, cleansed by Him. And if you are to serve Him, you must be cleansed.

The busiest place in the tabernacle, apparently, was not the brazen altar but the brazen laver. I have a notion that many of the priests got tired of going there. I can well understand that a couple of priests would meet there someday, one washing his feet and the other washing his hands. And one says to the other, "Don't you get tired of coming here?" I think the other one would answer, "Yes, this is wearisome, isn't it? You can't do anything in this tabernacle without washing. You can't offer sacrifice, you can't go in and serve God, you can't even move in here without washing. I've been up here now half a dozen times already today, and I have dish pan hands. Look at them. Washing, washing, washing."

God was teaching that if you are to come into His presence, this matter of sin has to be taken care of, and it must be taken care of adequately. There must be cleansing of the heart and of the life. Through the centuries this ritual had been handed down in Israel. Now, even in the homes, they had these waterpots that were there for nothing in the world but ceremonial cleansing.

I do not know this, but I rather suspect that when they got ready for the wedding, that these waterpots were not going to be used. They had already been used probably more than anything else about the place, and I think the lady of the house said, "For goodness sake, before the guests arrive, let's push them around to the back and try to cover them with something. We don't want the guests to see these old beaten, battered waterpots." They were just not to be seen at a wedding. But isn't it interesting what finally occupied center stage—waterpots. What is the most important thing in a wedding after all? Well, there may be some difference of opinion, but I learned a long time ago that actually it's what the bride wears. It's been my happy privilege to have several hundred young couples stand before me, and I go through the same ceremony each time. In fact it has become really a ritual with me. But I've observed this: When I come out with the bridegroom and the best man, there's very little stir. No one even smiles at the groom but his mother. I've often thought that it would be well if he could stay home; he's really not needed at a wedding at all. But when the bride comes in, that's when the important part takes place. When she comes down the aisle, everyone is looking, and they all want to see what the bride is wearing.

Would you tell me what the bride wore here? In fact, I do not know whether the bride was even present, because she's not even mentioned. I'm sure the society editor of the *Cana Chronicle* the next day must have had an elaborate article on what the bride wore, but the Word of God has nothing concerning it.

What are mentioned are six stone waterpots that had been pushed aside. Now the Lord Jesus says, "Bring them out in the open." And they become the most important thing at the wedding.

Notice the technique He uses, for I believe this is the technique that's very important for us today. "Jesus saith unto them, Fill the waterpots with water. And they filled them up to the brim." Those empty, battered, beaten waterpots represent you and me. This is where God begins with us. His first step was to fill the pots with water. Then "he saith unto them, Draw some out now, and bear it unto the governor of the feast. And they bore it." He begins with empty waterpots.

Today we hear a great deal about the Lord taking us and using us. I do not believe He can use anyone until he becomes an empty waterpot. I'm not sure I go along with the song "All for Jesus." What do you mean, all for Jesus? Even when He gets all, what does He get? He gets nothing. All for Jesus, as far as Vernon McGee is concerned, is nothing. Martin Luther put it in his quaint way: "God creates out of nothing. Therefore, until a man is nothing, God can make nothing out of him." He starts with an empty waterpot.

Often we hear preached: Let's bring our talents to the Lord. We have a notion today that we've got something to offer to God. I do not want to be ugly and unkind, but I do want to say that you have nothing God has to have. You have nothing that God needs.

I had the privilege of teaching the Hollywood Christian Group for several series in the group's early days. In those days they really were seeing conversions, and it was their practice to have a testimony at every meeting. I never shall forget one night a young couple got up who had just been converted out of nightclub entertainment. I must confess that they were as attractive and talented as any young couple I have ever seen. They had personality plus. They were beautiful people. In their testimony they told about how they had been nightclub entertainers, and now they wanted to give everything to the Lord. They wanted to take this wonderful talent and ability they had and use it for the Lord.

I just didn't like that way of putting it; so, after the service was over and we were sitting around having coffee and cake together, I became acquainted with that young couple, and they've been close friends of mine ever since. I said to them, "In your testimony tonight you mentioned that you have talent and ability, and I can see that you do. But I'd like to ask you, 'What kind of talent and ability that you can use in a nightclub can God use?'" They thought it over for a minute and then admitted that they really couldn't think of what it would be. Then I told them, "Frankly, when any of us come to God, we bring Him nothing—absolutely nothing. That's what we are. We're nothing." And I used this illustration: "When the Lord Jesus wanted to bring joy and blessing to that wedding in Cana, He began with empty waterpots, and when He uses you and me, He'll have to start with empty waterpots."

I don't think they were happy about it at the time, but

they're very good friends of mine today. I met them a couple of years ago on the streets of a city in the East, and when they started toward me, they called, "Here come a couple of empty water pots." God has used them in a very wonderful way.

May I say to you tonight that He wants to start with us as empty waterpots. That's where He's always begun with men of the past that He's used. Ephraem Syrus wrote years ago: "I pronounce my life wretched because it is unprofitable." Think that over for awhile. In this day when we hear so much about giving Jesus our all, we give Him nothing when we bring ourselves to Him. He starts with an empty waterpot.

Listen to David Brainerd, mightily used of God in this country among the Indians: "Oh, that my soul were holy, as He is holy. Oh, that it were pure, as Christ is pure, and perfect as my Father in heaven is perfect. These are the sweetest commands in God's Book comprising all others. And shall I break them? Must I break them? Am I under necessity of it as long as I live in the world? Oh, my soul, woe, woe is me, that I am a sinner."

When I came to Christ, all He got was just that much sin. That's all. I do not know you friends tonight very well, but I believe I can say that that's all He gets when He gets you. We bring Him nothing. Empty waterpots. But the wonder of wonders is what He can do with an empty waterpot—that is, if it's really empty and if it's brought to Him.

"Jesus saith unto them, Fill the waterpots with water. And they filled them up to the brim." That is the next step. And the water is the Word of God. It's so used again and again in Scripture. It's interesting that it was down at the water gate that Ezra put his pulpit to read the Word of God to the people, many of whom had never heard it before (Neh. 8). It was water to their souls. David spoke of the Word as being water to his soul, and the apostle Paul tells us we are washed by the water of the Word (Eph. 5:26). The Word of God is water. Our Lord begins with an empty waterpot and His second step is to fill us with the Word of God.

I'm not saying this because I'm here at Moody Bible Institute, but I have always thanked God for the Bible institute movement. It has done more to teach the Word of God to people in this country than any other movement. Thank God that Moody Bible Institute is still in that business. I believe that for anyone to be used of God today, the most important thing he must do is to get the water of the Word in him.

I love the way John put it here: "They filled them up to the brim." You can't get too much of the Word of God. Today the most important thing in the world for us to get into our hearts and lives is the Word of God. Now don't misunderstand me. I do not despise methods, and I do not despise gadgets, but it's the Word that God uses. The only thing He can and will use in an empty waterpot is the water put in there.

Now notice the next step that is taken here. "He saith unto them, Draw some out now, and bear it unto the governor of the feast. And they bore it. When the ruler of the feast had tasted the water that was made wine, and knew not from whence it was (but the servants who drew the water knew), the governor of the feast called the bridegroom. . . ." Our Lord said, "Draw out the water," and when it got to the bridegroom it was wine. Somewhere between the waterpot and the bridegroom, it became wine. Where? I can't answer that question. I do not know. I'm of the opinion that when it left the waterpot it was water. When it reached the bridegroom and the guests, it was wine. Our Lord did not take a little wand and wave it over the waterpots and say, "Hocus-pocus, abracadabra." He did nothing like that. He said to the servants, "Draw it out," and they drew it out, and it was apparently water. But when it was received by the guests, it was wine.

You just can't deal with this miracle without mentioning this because the question always comes up—was this intoxicating? I like the way Richard Cranshaw put it: "The conscious water saw its God and blushed." If you take the position that one of these modern theologians has taken, that our Lord was running a brewery, you've missed the entire import of the message. There's nothing as slanderous and blasphemous as that. To begin with, you must understand that wine was used in all the Levitical ceremonies. The drink offering was always included. When the drink offering was poured upon the burnt offering, it would just ascend as vapor and disappear. That's what Paul meant when he said to the Philippians that he wanted his life to be poured out. He wanted his life to be a drink offering poured out upon the burnt offering, which is Christ. And his life was lived out just like that—just like a drink offering poured on the offering of Christ. The drink offering of wine was a very important part of the Levitical priesthood.

Wine was also a staple part of the diet in that day. However, our Lord condemned drunkenness. The Word of God condemns drunkenness. By no stretch of the imagination can you say that my Lord was running a cocktail hour at the wedding at Cana of Galilee. These were a very religious people, and there's no thought of drunkenness here or anywhere. You just can't read that into this account, for it is not here.

Wine in the Scripture does represent joy. You find this in the book of Proverbs, for instance. It was used as a medicine. And Paul contrasted the use of wine with the filling of the Spirit: "Be not drunk with wine in which is excess, but be filled with the Spirit" (Eph. 5:18). So the wine speaks of the joy that only the Spirit of God can bring.

The picture we have here is that of an empty waterpot filled with water, and somewhere between the waterpot and the recipient, the water becomes the wine of joy. The water of the Word becomes salvation. I believe one of the great miracles taking place today is what the Word of God will do when it leaves lips of clay and reaches the heart of some lost, downcast individual. The Word of God can bring joy into that heart and life.

About a year ago we changed the format of our radio program. We're now running a through-the-Bible program. As far as we know it's a new concept in religious broadcasting—going through the Bible in two and a half years, over about fifty stations. I learned something when we began the new format. I found I could not use my clever alliterations, my beautiful verbage. And it was difficult to drag in a lot of my pet theories. All I could do was just give the Word of God. This frightened me because, frankly, I guess I didn't have very much faith. I thought the Lord had to have something from me—that there had to be something added to the Word of God. I say this for the glory of God—our mail has increased 150 percent. In one month more people have written to tell us they have accepted Christ than we saw in five years before that. I'm amazed at what an empty waterpot with just a little of the Word of God going out can accomplish for Him.

I believe that the crying need of the hour is for God to get hold of a few empty waterpots, fill them with the water of the Word and then get it ladled out to these parched, discouraged, distraught human beings that are about us today.

Now notice, "When the ruler of the feast had tasted the water that was made wine, and knew not whence it was (but the servants which drew the water knew), the governor of the feast called the bridegroom, and saith unto him, Every man at the beginning doth set forth good wine and, when men have well drunk, then that which is worse: but thou hast kept the good wine until now." Don't try to read into that that this is intoxicating liquor because he kept the good until now. After all, He just made it, and when you just make it, it's not wine. It's not intoxicating. You have to let it stand around for awhile before it becomes intoxicating.

Reserving the good until the last is the reverse of the usual procedure followed today. I've noticed that when my wife and I invite the young people for an evening, she goes to a wonderful Swedish bakery and buys some very good cookies to serve them. But because you never know how many young people are coming or how many they are going to eat, she always goes by the market and picks up a whole bag of hard cookies to have on hand, just in case she needs them. I mean they are really hard cookies; you'd have to have a hammer to break them. So when the young people finish the good cookies from the bakery, she gets out the hard cookies. Isn't that your method today, ladies, to always save the worst until the last? You never save the best until the last. The young people always seem to like those hard cookies better than the good ones, by the way. But the good cookies were given first, and the bad cookies were held back. The bridegroom here is being reminded that there has been a reversal of a common practice, and that is all.

"This beginning of miracles did Jesus in Cana, of Galilee." There is a church today which teaches that when Jesus was a boy, He performed miracles—that when He played with other little boys down in the land of Egypt, for example, they would make clay pigeons, and He would touch them and they would fly away. How do I know that's not true? Because it says here, "This beginning of miracles did Jesus in Cana, of Galilee." This is His first one.

The important statement is, " . . . and [he] manifested forth his glory; and his disciples believed on him." He did not perform this miracle for public display. He didn't perform it for the crowd or for the mob or for the religious rulers in Jerusalem. It's at the beginning of His ministry, He has just called these men, and it is for their benefit.

I believe today that when you and I are willing to become empty waterpots and recognize that we bring nothing to Him, we have nothing to bring, He will take us empty waterpots and fill us with the water of the Word of God and perform miracles. And He will show forth His glory. How many of us today in the Lord's service need to see His glory. May God help us to become empty waterpots in such a way that we can behold His glory.

May I?

Charles Haddon Spurgeon (1834–1892) was undoubtedly the most famous minister of the nineteenth century. Converted in 1850, he united with the Baptists and soon began to preach in various places. He became pastor of the Baptist church in Waterbeach in 1851, and three years later he was called to the decaying Park Street Church, London. Within a short time the work began to prosper, a new church was built and dedicated in 1861, and Spurgeon became London's most popular preacher. In 1855, he began to publish his sermons weekly; today they make up the fifty-seven volumes of *The Metropolitan Tabernacle Pulpit*. He founded a pastor's college and several orphanages.

This sermon is taken from *The Metropolitan Tabernacle Pulpit*, Volume 30.

Charles Haddon Spurgeon

2

MAY I?

If I may (Matthew 9:21).

THE WOMAN IN the narrative was fully persuaded that if she did but touch our Lord's garment she would be made whole. What she had heard and seen concerning Jesus made her sure of His superabundant power to heal the sick. A touch would do it. Yes, even a touch of His clothes. Her one and only question was, might she touch Him? Could she touch Him? She would surely be healed if she could touch; but was this allowable? Was this possible? I know that multitudes of sin-sick men and women are vexed with this same question. Oh, that I could help them over the difficulty! May the Holy Spirit, the Comforter, aid me!

This poor diseased woman did not utter this *if* of hers with her lips. Perhaps if she had it might not have troubled her so much, for a silent doubt usually eats right into the heart. You have heard of the Spartan boy who had hidden a fox in his bosom, and allowed it to eat into his vitals before he would own to it. Beware of having a doubt hidden away in your heart, gnawing and tearing. If you are even now suffering from "If I may, if I may," reveal the trouble to some tender Christian friend and you may soon escape from it.

But the sufferer now before us had the courage to put the question to a practical issue; she tried whether she might or not. She had the good sense, the grace-given wisdom, not to wait until she had solved that question in her mind, but she went and solved it, as a matter of fact, whether she might or not: she went and actually touched the hem of the garment of the Savior, and she was made perfectly whole. Oh that those I am now addressing would have the bravery and the earnestness to do the same! Oh, that they would put the disturbing question to a practical test at once! There can be but one result, for as many as touched Him were made perfectly whole.

Now, I know that souls are going to be saved tonight. Who they are I cannot tell; but some are certain to come to the Savior, and this night to be made perfectly whole. I know it because we prayed an hour ago for it downstairs, many of us, and we felt the assurance that we were heard. My dear son, in praying just now, I am sure felt a very remarkable liberty at the mercy seat, and the witness of the Spirit within that he was heard. The Lord has heard the petitions which we have presented in the name of Jesus. You are going to be saved. I would to God every unconverted person here would lean forward and say, "May it be *me*. God grant that salvation may come to *me*." I am going, therefore, in the simplest way possible, without any attempt at a sermon, to try to talk so as to meet this rankling question which lies within, festering and irritating many an earnest heart—this doubtful inquiry, "If I may."

You know, many of you, who Jesus is, and you believe Him to be the Son of God, the Savior of men. You are sure that "he is able to save them to the uttermost that come unto God by him." You have no doubt about those eternal verities which surround His Godhead, His birth, His life, His death, His resurrection, and His Second Advent.

The doubt is concerning yourself personally—"If I may be a partaker of this salvation." You feel quite certain that faith in Jesus Christ will save anyone—will save you if you exercise it. You have no doubt about the doctrine of justification by faith. You have learned it, and you have received it as a matter beyond all dispute, that he that believes in Him has ever lasting life; and you know that him that comes to Him He will in nowise cast out.

You know the remedy, and believe in its efficacy; but then comes the doubt—may I be healed by it? At the back of your belief in faith hides the gloomy thought, "May I believe? May I trust? I see the door is open: many are entering. May I? I see that there is washing from the worst of sins in the sacred fount. Many are being cleansed. May I wash and be clean?" Without formulating a doubt so as to express it, it comes up in all sorts of ways, and robs you of all comfort, and, indeed, of all hope. When a sermon is preached it is like as when one sets a table out with all manner of dainties, and you look at it, but do not feel that you have any right to sit down and partake. This is a wretched delusion. Its result will be deadly unless you are delivered from it. Like a harpy it preys upon you, croaking evermore.

When you see the brooks flowing with their sparkling streams, and you are thirsty, does there arise the thought in your heart that you are not permitted to drink? If so, you are out of your mind; you talk and think like one bereft of reason. Yet many are in this state spiritually. This doubting your liberty to come to Jesus is a very wretched business; it mars and spoils your reading and your hearing and your attempts to pray; and you will never get any comfort until this question has been answered in your heart once for all—"May I?"

Our Authorized Version may not be exactly correct in this passage, but I do not care whether it is or not, so far as my address is concerned, for it does not depend upon the accuracy of a text. I am quite satisfied to preach from it tonight; but there is another translation in the Revised Version, which I dare say is more accurate. I will preach from that when I have done with the first. This shall be our subject—"If I may"; or first, *"if I may be allowed,"* secondly, *"if I may be enabled,"* thirdly, *"if I actually do."* This last is the Revised Version: "If I do but touch the hem of his garment I shall be made whole."

If I May Be Allowed

First, take it as we have got it here: "If I may be allowed, or permitted, to touch the hem of his garment, I shall be made whole." That is your difficulty, is it?— whether you have liberty and warrant to come and trust Christ—whether you, such a sinner as you are, are permitted to repose your soul upon His great atonement and His finished work. Let me reason with you a little.

In the first place, you are quite sure of this—that *there is nothing to forbid your coming and resting your guilty soul upon Christ.* I shall defy you, if you will read all the Old and New Testament through, to put your finger upon a single verse in which God has said that you may not come and put your trust in Christ. Perhaps you will reply that you do not expect to read it in the Bible, but God may have said it somewhere where it is not recorded.

Well, I answer you there; for He says, "I have not spoken in secret, in a dark place of the earth: I said not unto the seed of Jacob, Seek ye me in vain." Now, He has bidden you over and over again to seek His face, but He has never said that you shall seek His face in vain. Dismiss that thought.

Again I return to what I have said: there is nothing in the Scripture that refuses you permission to come and repose your soul once for all upon Christ. It is written, "Whosoever will, let him take the water of life freely." Does that exclude you? It is written, "Whosoever shall call upon the name of the Lord shall be saved." Does that shut you out? No, it includes you; it invites you; it encourages you. And I come again to what I have said—that nowhere in the Word of God is it written that you will be cast out if you come, or that Jesus Christ will not remove your burden of sin if you come and lay it at His feet.

Ah, no; a thousand passages of Scripture welcome you, but not one stands with a drawn sword to keep you back from the tree of life. Our heavenly Father sets His angels at the gates of His house to welcome all comers; but there are no dogs to bark at poor beggars, nor so much as a notice that trespassers must beware. Come and welcome. There is none to say to you no.

Further, do you not think that *the very nature of the Lord Jesus Christ should forbid your raising a doubt about your being permitted to come and touch His garment's hem?* Surely, if anyone were to paint the Lord Jesus Christ as an ascetic, repelling with lofty pride the humbler folk who had never reached His dignity of consecration—if any were to paint Him as a Pharisee driving off publicans and sinners, or as an iceberg of righteousness chilling the sinful, it would be a foul slander upon His divine character. If anyone were to say that Jesus Christ is exacting—that He will not receive to Himself the guilty just as they are, but requires a great deal of them, and will only welcome to Himself those who are, like Himself, good, and true, and excellent, that would not be truth but the direct opposite of it; for, "this man receiveth sinners, and eateth with them," was thrown in His face when He lived here below; and what the prophet said of Him was most certainly true, if anything was ever true. "A bruised reed shall he not break, and the smoking flax shall he not quench."

Little children are wonderful judges of character; they know intuitively who is kind. And so are loving women. They do not go through the processes of reasoning, but they come to a conclusion very soon as to a man's personal character. Now, the children came and clambered our Redeemer's knee, and the mothers brought their infants for His blessing. How can you dream that He will repel *you*?

The women wept and bewailed Him; whoever might refuse Him they pitied him, and therefore I am sure that He is not hard to move. Therefore I want you to feel sure of this—that there is nothing in the Savior's character which can for a moment lead Him to discard you and to drive you from His presence. Those who know Him best will say that it is impossible for Him ever to refuse the poor and needy. Not a blind man could cry to Him without receiving sight, nor a hungry man look to Him without being fed. He was touched with a feeling of our infirmities—the most gentle and loving and tender of all that ever dwelt upon this earth.

I pray you, then, take it for granted that you may come boldly to Him without fear of a rebuff. If He has power to heal you when you touch Him, rest assured that you may touch Him. You may believe; there is no question; for Jesus is too loving to refuse you. It will give the Lord Jesus joy to receive you. It is not possible that He should say no to you: it is not in His nature to spurn you from His presence.

Will you think, yet again, of *the fullness of Christ's power to save*, and make a little argument of it. Christ was so full of power to bless that the secret virtue even saturated His clothes. It overflowed His blessed person; it ran down to the skirts of His garments; aye, and it went to that blue hem which every Jew wore round about his dress—that fringe of blue. It went into that border so that if the woman did but touch the ravelings of His garment, virtue would stream into her. If the touch was a touch of faith it mattered not where the contact was made.

Well now, you often judge of a man's willingness to help by the power that He has. When a person has little to give he is bound to be economical in his giving. He must look at every penny before he gives it, if he has so few pence to spare. But when a nobleman has no limit to his estate you feel sure that he will freely give if his heart be generous and tender. The blessed Lord is so full of healing power that He cannot need to stint Himself as to the miracles of healing He shall work; and He must be, according to the goodness of His nature, delighted to overflow, glad to communicate to those who come.

You know if a city is straitened for water the corporation will send out an order that only so much may be used, and there is a stinting of public baths, and factories, because there is a scarcity of the precious fluid. But if you go along the Thames when we have had a rainy season, you laugh at the notion of a short supply and economical rules. If a dog wants to drink from a river, nobody ever questions his right to do so. He comes down to the water and he laps, and, what is more, he runs right into it, regardless of those who may have to drink after him. Look at the cattle, how they stand knee-deep in the stream and drink, and drink again; and nobody ever says, as he goes up the Thames, that those poor London people will run short of water, for the dogs and the cattle are drinking it up before it gets down to London. No, it never enters our heads to petition the conservators to restrain the dogs and the cows; for there is so much water that there must be full liberty to everyone to drink to the full.

Your question is, "May I? May I?" I answer that question by this: there is nothing to forbid you; there is everything in the nature of Christ to encourage you; and there is such a fullness of mercy in Him that you cannot think that He can have the slightest motive for withholding His infinite grace.

Moreover, suppose you come to Christ as this woman came, and touch the hem of His garment, *you will not injure Him.* You ought to hesitate in getting good to yourself if you would injure the person through whom you obtain that good. But you will not injure the Lord Jesus Christ. He perceived that virtue had gone out of Him, but He did not perceive it by any pain He felt—for rather do I believe that He perceived it by the pleasure which it caused Him. Something gave Him unusual joy. A faith touch had reached Him through His clothes, and He rejoiced to respond by imparting healing virtue from Himself.

You will not defile my Lord, O sinner, if you bring Him all your sin. He will not have to die again to put away your fresh burden of transgression. He will not have to shed one drop of blood to make atonement for your multiplied sin: the one sacrifice on Calvary anticipated all possible guiltiness. If you will come just as you are, He will not have to leave heaven again, and be born again on earth, and live another sorrowful life in order to save you. He will not need to wear another crown of thorns, or bear another wound in His hands, or feet, or side. He has done all His atoning work. Do you not remember His victorious cry—"It is finished"?

You cannot injure Him though all your injurious thoughts, and words, and speeches be laid upon Him. You will not be robbing Him of anything though your faith touch should convey a life into yourself. He has such a fullness about Him that if all you poor sinners will come at once, when you have taken away all of merit that you need, there will be as much merit left as there was before. When you deal with the infinite you may divide and subtract, but you cannot diminish. If the whole race were washed in the infinite fountain of Jesus' merit, the infinite would still remain.

Let me tell you that if you come to Jesus and just trust Him tonight—only trust Him—*you shall rather benefit Him than injure Him*; for it is His heart's joy to forgive sinners. He longs and thirsts to heal wounded

consciences. My Lord is hungering, even now that He is
in heaven, to bring poor sinners to His Father's feet, and
reconcile them to Him; so you will bless Him, you will
increase His joy, if you will return to the great Father
whose house you have left. You will delight His heart as
again He finds the lost piece of money, bears back the
lost sheep, and welcomes home the returning prodigal. I
think you need not keep on saying "If I may"; for these
cheering reasons ought to convince you that you are fully
warranted to trust in Him whom God has set forth to be
a prince and a Savior, to give repentance to Israel, and
remission of sins.

Might not this also help you? *Others just like you have
ventured to Him, and there has not been a case in which
they have been refused.* I thought, like you, when I was a
child, that the Gospel was a very wonderful thing, and
free to everybody but myself. I should not have wondered
at all if my brother and sisters as well as my father and
mother had been saved; but, somehow, I could not get a
hold of it myself. It was a precious thing, quite as much
out of my reach as the queen's diamonds. So I thought.

To many the Gospel is like a tramcar in motion, and
they cannot jump upon it. I thought surely everybody
would be saved, but I would not; and yet, soon after I
began to cry for mercy I found it. My expectations of
difficulty were all sweetly disappointed. I believed and
found immediate rest to my soul. When I once understood
that there was life in a look at the crucified One, I gave
that look, and I found eternal life. Hitherto I have never
met with anybody who did give that look and was re-
pulsed; but they all say,

> I came to Jesus as I was,
> Weary and worn and sad;
> I found in him a resting place,
> And he has made me glad.

Nobody ever bears a contrary witness. I challenge the
universe to produce a man who was chased from Christ's
door, or forbidden to find in Him a Savior. I pray you,
therefore, observe that, since others have come this way

to life and peace, God has appointed it to be the common thoroughfare of grace. Poor guilty sinners, there is a mark set up, "This way for sinners. This way for the guilty. This way for the hungry. This way for the thirsty. This way for the lost. Come unto me, all ye that labor and are heavy laden, and I will give you rest." Why, surely, you need not say, "If I may."

And why do you think—and that is one more question I would put to you: *why do you think that the Lord Jesus Christ in His mercy has led you here tonight?* "Oh, I always come," says one. Then what has induced you always to come where Christ is talked about so much, and where He saves so many? Surely the Lord means to accept you if you will believe on Jesus!

"But I do not come here usually," says one; "I only stepped in here tonight, I am afraid, out of curiosity." Yes, curiosity moved you; but may it not be that compassion moved God to guide you here? I like to hear a wife say, "My husband is not a member of the church, sir, but he comes to hear the Gospel, and therefore I have hope of him." Aye, yes; if we get them into the battle a shot will come their way one of these days.

I love to see you hungry sparrows round about the window; you will get courage enough to pick up a crumb of mercy one of these days. I hope so. And why should it not be now? If the trouble is "If I may," I will ask you whether it does not help to remove that trouble to reflect that you are still on praying ground and pleading terms with God. You might long before this have been cast into despair. Should not the Lord's long-suffering lead you to repentance, and induce you to come to Christ?

Now listen, friend: there is no room to say "If I may," for, first of all, *you are invited* to come and accept Christ as your Savior—invited over and over again in the Word of God. "The Spirit and the bride say, Come. And let him that heareth say, Come. And let him that is athirst come. And whosoever will, let him take the water of life freely." "Ho, everyone that thirsts, come to the waters, and he that has no money; come, buy, and eat; yes, come, buy wine and milk without money and without price." Jesus

Christ invites all those that labor and are heavy laden to come to Him, and He will give them rest.

God is honest in His invitations. Be you sure of that. If God invites you, He desires you to come and accept the invitation. After reading the many invitations of the Word of God to such as you are, you may not say "If I may." It will be a wicked questioning of the sincerity of God.

In addition to being invited, *you are entreated.* Many passages of Scripture go far beyond a mere invitation. God persuades and entreats you to come to Him. He seems to cry as one that weeps, "As I live, saith the Lord God, I have no pleasure in the death of the wicked; but that the wicked turn from his way and live: turn ye, turn ye; for why will ye die, O house of Israel?" Our Lord and Master when He made the feast, and they that were bidden did not come, sent out His servants to compel them to come in. He used more than a bare invitation, He put forth a divine compulsion.

I would entreat, persuade, exhort all of you who have not believed in Jesus to do so now. In the name of Jesus, I beseech you, seek the Lord. I do not merely put it to you, "Will you or will you not?" but I would lay my whole heart by the side of the request and say to you, "Come to Jesus. Come and rest your guilty souls on Him." Do you not understand the Gospel message? Do you know what it asks and what it gives? You shall receive perfect pardon in a moment if you believe in Jesus. You shall receive a life that will never die—receive it now, quick as a lightning flash, if you do but trust in the Son of God. Whoever you may be, and whatever you may have done, if you will with your heart believe in Him whom God has raised from the dead, and obey Him henceforth as your Lord and Savior, all manner of sin and of iniquity shall be forgiven to you. God will blot out your iniquities like a cloud. He will make you begin *de novo*—afresh, anew. A new creature in Christ Jesus will He make you. Old things shall pass away and all things become new.

But there is the point—believing in Jesus; and you look me in the face and cry, "But may I?" May you? Why, you are exhorted, invited, entreated to do so. Nor is this all.

You are even commanded to do it. This is the command-ment—that you believe on Jesus, whom He has sent. This is the Gospel, "He that believeth and is baptized shall be saved; but he that believeth not shall be damned." There is a command, with a threatening for disobedience. Shall anybody say "May I" after that? If I read, "Thou shalt love the Lord thy God with all thy heart," do I say, "May I love God?" If I read, "Honor thy father and thy mother," do I say, "May I honor my father and my mother?" No. A command is a permit and something more. It gives full allowance and much more. As you will be damned if you believe not, you have herein given to you a right to believe—not only a permission, but a warrant of the most practical kind. Oh, can you not see it? Will you not cry to God, "Lord, if You will damn me if I do not believe, You have in this given me a full Gospel liberty to believe. Therefore I come and put my trust in Jesus."

"If I may"—why, I think that this questioning ought to come to an end now. Will you not give it up? May the Holy Spirit show you, poor sinner, that you may now lay your burden down at Jesus' feet, and be at once saved. You may believe. You have full permission now to confess your sin and to receive immediate pardon: see if it be not so. Cast your guilty soul on Him, and rise forgiven and renewed, henceforth to live in fervent gratitude, a miracle of love.

That is the first meaning of the text: "If I may be per-mitted to touch the hem of his garment, I shall be made whole."

If I May Be Enabled?

But then there arises in other hearts this equally bitter question, "But can I? I know that I may if I can; but I cannot." This woman, seeing the press, might have said, "If I can touch the hem of His garment, I shall be made whole; but can I get at Him? Can a feeble person like me force my way through the throng and touch Him?"

Now, that is the question I am going to answer. The will to believe in Christ is as much a work of grace as faith itself, and where the will is given and a strong desire, a measure of grace is already received, and with it the power to believe. Do you not know that the will to commit adultery is, according to Scripture, reckoned as adultery? "He hath committed adultery with her already in his heart." Now, if the very thought of uncleanness and the will toward it is the thing itself, then a desire or will to believe contains within itself the major part of faith. I say not that it is all, but I do say this—that if the power of God has made a man will to believe, the greater work has been done, and his actually believing will follow in due course. That entire willingness to believe is nine-tenths of believing.

Inasmuch as to will is present with you, the power which you find not as yet will certainly come to you. The man is dead, and the hardest thing is to make him live; but in the case before us the quickening is accomplished, for the man lives so far as to will: he wills to believe, he yearns to believe, he longs to believe: how much has been done for him! Rising from the dead is a greater thing than the performance of an act of life. Already I see some breathings of life in you who are longing and yearning to lay hold on Christ. You shall yet lay hold on Him, and live in His presence.

I would have said to that woman, had I been there and known then what I know now, "Oh, woman, that faith of yours, that if you can but touch the hem of His garment you will be made whole, is a greater thing than the actual touch can be. It is not at present so operative, but it is a more singular product of grace. You have within you already the greater work of grace, and the less will follow. A thousand persons could press through the crowd and touch the hem of the Savior's robe, but you are the only person in whom God has wrought the faith that a touch will make you whole. I might say of such a faith as that, 'flesh and blood hath not revealed it unto thee'; and if you are in that condition, there is a very great work done in you already, and you need not doubt the possibility of your touching the sacred vesture."

But mark this, faith in Christ is the simplest action that anybody ever performs. It is the action of a child;

indeed, it is the action of a newborn babe in grace. A newborn babe never performs an action that is very complicated. We say, "Oh, it is such a babyish thing," meaning thereby that it is so small. Now, faith comes at the moment that the child is born into God's family; it is coeval with the new birth. One of the first signs and tokens of being born again is faith; therefore it must be a very, very simple thing. I venture to put it very plainly when I say that faith in Christ differs in no respect from faith in anybody else, except as to the person upon whom that faith is set. You believe in your mother; you may in the same manner believe in Jesus Christ, the Son of God. You believe in your friend; it is the same act that you have to do toward your higher and better Friend. You believe the news that is commonly reported and printed in the daily journals; it is the same act which believes the Scripture, and the promise of God.

The reason why faith in the Lord Jesus is a superior act to faith in anyone else lies in this fact—that it is a superior person whom you believe in, and superior news that you believe; and your natural heart is more averse to believing in Jesus than to believing in anyone else. The Holy Spirit must teach your faith to grasp the high things of Christ Jesus; but that grasp is by the hand of a simple childlike faith. But it is the same faith; mark you that.

It is the gift of God in so far as this—that God gives you the understanding and the judgment to exercise it upon His Son, and to receive Him. The faith of a child in his father is almost always a wonderful faith; just that faith we would ask for our Lord Jesus. Many a child believes that there is no other man in the world so great and good, and right and kind and rich, and everything else as his father is; and if anybody were to say that his father was not as wonderful a man as Mr. Gladstone, or some other great statesman, he would become quite grieved; for if his father is not king, it is a mistake that he is not. Children think so of their parents, and that is the kind of faith we would have you exercise toward the Lord Jesus Christ, who deserves such confidence, and much more.

We should give to Jesus a faith by which we do Him honor and magnify Him exceedingly. As the child never thinks where the bread and butter is to come from tomorrow morning, and it never enters its little head to fret about where it will get new socks when the present ones are worn out, so must you trust in Jesus Christ for everything you want between here and heaven—trust Him without asking questions. He can and will provide. Just give yourself up to Him entirely, as a child gives itself up to a parent's care, and feels itself to be at ease.

Oh, what a simple act it is—this act of faith. I am sure that it must be a very simple act, and cannot require wisdom, and so forth, because I notice that it is the wise people that cannot do it; it is the strong people that cannot do it; it is the people who are righteous in themselves that cannot reach it. Faith is a kind of act which is performed by those who are childlike in heart, whom the world calls fools and ridicules and persecutes for their folly. "Not many wise men after the flesh, not many mighty, not many noble, are called: but God hath chosen the weak things of the world and base things, and things which are despised hath God chosen." There are persons with no education whatever, who just know their Bibles are true, and have an abundant faith. They are poor in this world, but rich in faith. Happy people!

Alas, for those wise people whose wisdom prevents faith in Jesus! They have been to more than one university, and have earned all the degrees that carnal wisdom can bestow upon them, and yet they cannot believe in Jesus Christ, the Son of God. Oh, friend, do not think that faith is some difficult and puzzling thing, for then these senior wranglers and doctors of divinity would have it.

It is the simplest act that the mind can perform. Just as I lean now with all my weight on this rail, and if it breaks I fall; so lean your full weight on Jesus Christ, and that is faith. Just as a babe lies in its mother's bosom, unconscious of the thunderstorm, or of the rocking of the ship, quite safe and happy because it rests in the bosom of love; all fear and care laid aside because of that true heart which beats beneath: even so do you just

cast yourself altogether upon Christ, and that is all that
you have to do—just, in fact, to leave off doing.

> Cast thy deadly doing down,
> Down at Jesu's feet.
> Stand in him, in him alone,
> Gloriously complete.

"But shall I not have to do many good works?" says one.
You shall do as much as ever you like when you are once
saved; but in this matter of your salvation you must fling
all self-righteousness away as so much devilry that will
ruin and injure you, and come simply to Christ, and Christ
alone, and trust in Him.

"Oh," says one, "I think I see a little light. If I am
enabled—if I do but get power enough to trust in Jesus, I
shall be made whole." I will ask you another question. Do
you not know that you are bound to believe in Christ—
that it is due to Christ that He be believed in? I would not
make extensive claims upon your faith for myself.

Often have I said to friends who have told me that they
could not believe in Christ, "Could you believe in *me?* If I
were to tell you that I would do such and such things,
would you believe it?" "Oh yes, sir." "If anyone were to say
that he did not believe what I said, how would you feel?"
"I should feel very indignant, for I feel that I can trust
you; indeed I cannot help trusting you." When I receive
such confidence from one of my fellow creatures, I feel
that it is cruelly wrong for the same person to say, "I
cannot trust Christ." Oh, beloved, not believe Jesus! When
did He lie? "Oh, but I cannot trust Him." Not trust Him?
What madness is this? And did He die in very truth? Did
He seal His life's witness with His heart's blood; and can
you not believe Him?

My own conviction is that a great many of you can, and
that already, to a large extent, you do; only you are looking for signs and wonders which will never come. Why
not exert that power a little farther? The Spirit of God
has given to you a measure of faith; oh, believe more
fully, more unreservedly. Why, I know that you shivered
just now at the very thought of doubting Christ. You felt

how unjust and wrong it was; there is latent in you already a faith in Him. "He that believeth not God hath made him a liar." Would you make Christ a liar? Dear hearts, I know that you would not. Although you say that you dare not trust Him, yet you know that He is no liar, and you know that He is able to save you. What a strange state your mind has reached. How bewildered and befogged you are; for already I think, as a looker-on, I can see that there is within your soul a real faith in Jesus Christ; and yet what doubts distract you. Why not bring faith to the front and say, "I do believe, I will believe that the Christ who is the Son of the Highest, and who died for the guilt of men, is able to save those that trust Him, and therefore I trust Him to save me. Sink or swim I trust Him. Lost or saved I will trust Him. Just as I am, with no other plea but that I am sure that He is able and willing to save, I cast my guilty soul on Him." You have the power to trust Jesus when you have already yielded to the conviction that He is worthy to be trusted. You have but to push to its practical conclusion what God the Holy Spirit has already wrought in many of you, and you will at once find peace.

Still, if you think that there is something that prevents your having faith in Christ, though you know that if you had it you would be saved, I do earnestly entreat you not to stay contentedly for a single hour without a full, complete, and saving faith in Christ; for if you die unbelievers you are lost, and lost forever. Your only safety lies in believing in the Lord Jesus Christ with all your heart, and obeying His commandments. Therefore use what common sense would suggest to you as the means for obtaining faith.

If I were told in the vestry after service something by a true friend whose word I could not doubt, and yet if what he said seemed incredible, I should express to him a wish to believe it. I would not wish to imply for a moment that he was not truthful; but somehow I find it difficult to believe the remarkable statement that he made. What should I do in the case?

If it was pressing that I should believe this statement, I would ask him, "How did you come by the information?

Where did you hear or read it? What are the precise facts?" Perhaps the moment that he mentioned where he got it from I should conclude at once that the wonderful statement was unquestionably correct. Or if he said, "Well, I give it to you on my own authority; but if you want any further information, you can get it by reading such and such a document: here is the document"—why, I would read it directly. I would read with a good deal of happy prejudice in favor of my faithful friend. Anyhow, I would read it to see whether I could fully believe what he said, because I would be sure that he would not intentionally deceive me. Now, if there be anything in the teaching of the Lord Jesus Christ, or anything about Him that you question, let me invite you to read over the four Gospels again, especially the story of His crucifixion. That Cross of His is a very wonderful thing, for not only does it save those who have faith in it, but it breeds faith in those who look at it.

> When I see him wounded, bleeding,
> Dying on th' accursed tree,
> Then I feel my heart believing
> That he suffered thus for me.

There is life in a look at Christ, because in the very considering of Christ there is the breeding of a living faith. We listen to the Word, and faith comes by hearing. We read the Word, and picture the whole thing before our eyes, and we say, "Yes, I do believe it. I never saw it quite in this fashion before, but I now believe it, and I will risk my soul on it."

Now, dear hearts, if any of you who have never trusted Christ will trust Him tonight, if you perish I will perish with you! For, though I have known my Lord these thirty-five years, I have no other hope of salvation than I had when I first came to Him. I had no merits of my own then, and I have none now. I have preached many sermons, offered many prayers, given much alms, brought many souls to Christ; but I place all that I ever have done under my feet, and desire, as far as it is good, to give to God the glory of it; but as far as it comes of myself, I would sink it in the sea. I am saved in Christ, by faith in Him; but confidence in myself is detestable to me. I dare believe in Jesus Christ as my all in all, but I am less than nothing before Him.

Come; we start fair, you see. If we start tonight, you and I will start on a level, with the same confidence in the same Savior, the same blood to cleanse us, and the same power to save us, and we will meet in heaven. As surely as we meet at the Cross, we will meet where the Savior wears the crown. Oh, that you would trust Him now, and believe Him. "I have no good works," says one. Then for certain you cannot trust in them. You will be forced to trust in Jesus only. "Oh, but I have no good feelings." I am glad to hear you say so. Then you are not tempted to trust in feelings, but will be drawn to trust wholly on your Lord. "Oh, but I feel so unfit." Very well, then you cannot trust in your fitness, but must trust in Him alone. It is a blessing when spiritual poverty forces a man into the way of life.

If I Actually Do?

Here I close with these words. This woman said in her heart, "If I do touch the hem of his garment, I shall"— what? "I shall be made whole." It is not "If I may but touch I *may be* made whole." No; she had got over the may be's in the first struggle. It is "If I may I shall." If you trust Christ you shall be made whole. If you do tonight actually repose yourself in Christ, as the Lord lives, you must live and be saved. Unless this Bible is all a lie, unless Jesus was a rank impostor, unless the eternal God can change, you that come and trust yourself with Jesus must and shall be saved in the last great day of account.

"Bold shall I stand in that great day," for I shall tell the Lord of His own promise, and how He bade me trust Him; and if I am not saved then His word is broken, and that can never be. He is true. Oh, it is this that some of you want to have done with—thinking, and talking, and considering, and hoping. You need now to come and trust, resting yourself fully and wholly on what Christ has done. He loved, and lived, and died that sinners might not die.

He wrought a complete work, of which He said as He expired, "It is finished." There is nothing for you to add to it, nothing for you to bring with you to make that work complete; but you yourself, stripped naked of every hope, black, foul, guilty, abominable, the worst of the worst, have only to come and look up to those five wounds, and to that bleeding, thorn-crowned head, and to say, "Into thy hands I commit my spirit," and you shall be saved. It is done. "Thy sins which are many are forgiven thee. Go, and sin no more." You are His child. Go and live to the glory of your Father; and may the peace of God that passes all understanding be with you forever and ever. Amen.

The Boat's Breadth

George H. Morrison (1866–1928) assisted the great
Alexander Whyte in Edinburgh, pastored two churches,
and then became pastor in 1902 of the distinguished
Wellington Church on University Avenue in Glasgow, Scotland. His preaching drew great crowds; in fact, people
had to line up an hour before the services to be sure to get
seats in the large auditorium. Morrison was a master of
imagination in preaching, yet his messages are solidly
biblical.

From his many published volumes of sermons, I have
chosen this message, found in *The Unlighted Lustre*, published in 1919 by Hodder and Stoughton, London.

George H. Morrison

3

THE BOAT'S BREADTH

Cast the net on the right side of the ship (John 21:6).

THERE ARE FEW scenes in the Gospel more impressive than this scene in the early morning by the sea of Galilee. Not even the meeting between Christ and Mary in the garden is more touching or tender than this incident. Calvary was past, the night of darkness was ended; Jesus had risen and the awful strain was over. It is in such hours that men instinctively turn again to the common toils which the strain has interrupted, and in such an hour Peter said "I go a-fishing." So Peter and his comrades toiled all night, but for all their toil, their fishing was a failure. Night—nothing— how these words chime together; night—nothing, morning— master. For in the morning the risen Christ stood by the lake, and cried to them "Children, have ye any meat?" There was only one answer to that straight question—it was No (we may be near to Christ, and yet be starving); then He said to them, "Cast the net on the right side of the ship." They cast it therefore, and it was filled with fish. Whereon in an instant the disciple whom Jesus loved, and to whom the love of Christ gave eyes like the eyes of an eagle, turned to his comrades and said, "It is the Lord."

The words, then, that I wish to dwell upon are these: Cast the net on the right side of the ship. And what do they suggest to me? These three important truths. First, what we long for is often nearer than we think. Second, we should never be afraid to change our methods. Third, Christ can manage things for us better than we can our- selves.

What We Long for Is Often Nearer Than We Think

You see at a glance that it was so that morning. Some- how, within the sweep of their nets, was the harvest of

the sea these men were looking for. All night they had
toiled without one sign of fish; they had lost heart, they
were weary, hungry, hopeless. "Ah!" they would whisper,
"this loch is sadly changed; there used to be good fish in
it, there doesn't seem one in it now." But the fish were
there, as plentiful as ever, nor were they far away in
remote bays and creeks: cast the net on the right side of
the ship—and it was full of great fishes, an hundred and
fifty and three. What they had toiled for all night was not
remote. What their hearts were set on was not far away.
When Peter and Thomas and John recalled that morning
amid the stress and the struggles of the after years, it
would flash on them as one of its sweetest memories that
what we long for may be nearer than we think.

Now often in reading the Bible I am struck with the
divine insistence on that truth. And I take it that when
God repeats a thing, He is bent on getting it graven on
our hearts. Let me only recall to you the case of Hagar,
when she fled with Ishmael under the taunts of Sarah.
Her flight lay through the desert with her child, and in
the desert her womanly strength gave out. There was no
water, there was no sign of water and her child was per-
ishing, and she cried to Abraham's God. And then and
there God opened Hagar's eyes and within a stone's cast
of her child there was a well. She would have given all
the world for water, and it was running near her all the
time. She thought of the well beside the tent of Abraham,
and there was a spring not a hundred yards away. And
the days would pass, and Hagar would reach Egypt; and
she would dwell among the temples of idolatry, but she
would remember, when all her hair was silvered, that the
things we long for may be nearer than we dream.

Every one of us needs to learn that lesson. We are so
prone to think that the best is inaccessible. But all that
we long for—happiness, love, peace, power—like the hundred and fifty fishes is just here. Ah, sirs, if all that we
craved for was remote, life would not be so tragic as it is.
If all that we craved for was very far away, the story of
humanity would be less pitiable. But the pity of a thousand lives is this, that love and joy and power and peace

are here, yet by the breadth of a fishing boat men some-how miss them, and all their lives they are toiling in the dark. It is easy to run away from home. It is not so easy to run away from self. Believe that the kingdom of heaven is within you. Believe that the best and the brightest is just here. The things that we crave for, without which we cannot live, which make all the difference between morn and midnight, these things are always nearer than we dream.

And if that is so of happiness and love you may be certain it is so of Christ: Peter and Nathanael and James and John made that discovery beside the lake. The scene was full of memories of Jesus: every light that twinkled on the loch shore recalled Him. I do not think one hour would pass that night, when the nets were shot and the fishing boat was rocking, but the name of Jesus would be on Peter's lips. They were longing for Him with a longing quite immeasurable; they missed Him unutterably, they could not live without Him. And they learned in the morn-ing when He stood on the shore and called them that the Christ they longed for was nearer than they thought. Do I speak to any who are longing for a Savior? To any who have toiled all night and have caught nothing? To any who are saying "My life is a sorry failure, although God knows I have struggled in the dark"? Behold! I stand at the door and knock, says Christ—the very power and presence that you need. It is easy to believe that Christ wrought in Galilee. It is easy to believe His power in the past. The hard thing is to believe that here and now there is One who can redeem and save and change you. Yet that is what you are longing for tonight. No one else knows it: they think you are quite satisfied. But you are not satisfied, and I am here to tell you that all that you long for is nearer than you dream.

We Should Never Be Afraid to Change Our Methods

But I pass on; in the second place, we should never be afraid to change our methods. Just think what would have happened by the lake if the disciples had been mastered by that cowardly fear. All night they had cast their nets on the left side—there may have been some fisherman's superstition in the matter—they were simply doing what they had been taught to do, they were holding fast to universal custom. Then in the morning came the ringing voice "Cast the net on the right side of the ship. Try a new method now. Adopt new plans. Strike out on a new course in the gray dawn." What a deal the disciples would have lost if they had sullenly refused to make that venture! No mighty fish would have filled their net to breaking. No one in the boat would have cried "It is the Lord." The figure would have vanished from the shore, the hot sun would have mounted; and a dreary day would have followed a weary night. But they cast their nets and everything was different. They altered their plans, and the day became divine. It was Christ who was near them; the Savior whom they loved. They had a day of royal fellowship with Him. And I think that in after years when Peter and James and John were fighting their Lord's battles in the world, as often as they recalled this scene in Galilee they would never be afraid to change their methods.

In our moral and spiritual lives we must get rid of this debasing fear. When we have been toiling all night and have caught nothing, it is time to cast the net upon the other side. Henry Drummond used to tell us of a duel that he had witnessed in one of the German universities. The combatants faced each other, and the swords made rapid play, and stroke after stroke was given, parried, baffled. Then suddenly, quick as a flash, one fighter changed his tactics; with the swiftness of thought he gave an unlooked-for stroke; and by the unlooked-for stroke the first blood was drawn. We are all fighting heavenward and Godward in a duel far more terrible than that of German students. There is not one of us in whom the flesh does not lust against the spirit, and the spirit against the flesh, and sometimes it seems as if victory were impossible. Try some new plan tonight. Strike out upon fresh lines. Have the courage to adopt a novel stroke. You have been fishing on the left and failing long enough. Cast the net on the right side of the ship.

Of course I would not have any one imagine that Jesus

is putting a premium upon fickleness. There is no more hopeless character in the world than that of the fickle and inconstant man. The very fact that all through the weary night the disciples had evidently fished on the left side, shows that in all of them there was that noble doggedness without which strong character is never forged. The man who can toil all night though he gets nothing is the rough material out of which saints are made. There is something heroic in all quiet persistency, especially when not one fish comes to the net. But to all of us, I imagine, there come mornings like the morning that dawned on these fishers at the lake; hours when we feel more intensely, when we see more vividly, when hopes are born in us and when new vistas open. It is in such hours, if we be men at all, that we will never hesitate to make great changes— we will cast our nets on the right side of the ship. We have never really prayed, but we shall pray now. We have never been thankful, we shall be thankful now. We have let devotion take the place of service, or we have let service take the place of prayer. Beware of the tyranny of habit in religion. There are ruts for the heart as well as for the wheels. We have toiled all night upon the left and have caught nothing. Cast the net on the right side of the ship.

And that is not only a lesson for the individual: it is a lesson for the whole church of Christ. I am no advocate of ill-considered changes. A mighty church must always be slow to move. I love old sanctuaries worn by the hand of time, and the grass-grown corners where our fathers sleep. I love to worship simply and in quiet places, where the leaves brush against the windows and the birds are singing, where there are rugged faces around me that have known what tears are; where I can bow in reverence before Almighty God. I love solemnity and dignity in worship. I love a church mellowed and gray with years. But the question of questions is not what I love. The question of questions is *what about the nets?* Are they full, are they empty, are there any fish in them? Are men being saved? Is the world being redeemed? If it is not, then let the dead past bury its dead, and cast the nets on the right side of

the ship. Do not be eager for a change of methods. Do not
be afraid of a change of methods. Measure the matter by
the nets, and the nets only—by the power of the church
with a dying and lost world.

> New occasions teach new duties,
>   Time makes ancient good uncouth,
> They must up and ever onward
>   Who would keep abreast of truth.

Christ Can Manage Our Daily Lives Better Than We Can Ourselves

In the third place I was to speak of this, that Christ can
manage our daily lives better than we can ourselves. But
the time has gone and I can only hint at it, for it is too
precious a matter to be wholly omitted. Now just think of
it, Peter and James were fishermen. They had been fall-
ing into that loch since they were babies. They knew every bay in it and every trick of the wind and every art and
secret of the fisherman's craft. Then Jesus came to them.
He gave directions. Did they resent it as gross interference? They did what He bade them, and doing it they
found that He could manage their business better than
they themselves.

Now after we have preached, businessmen sometimes
say, "Ah! the minister knows nothing about business."
That may be true, yet I should like to say in passing
that the more I know businessmen, the more I honor
them. In the face of risks we ministers know nothing of,
they show a courage and a patience that put some of us
to shame. I have felt a hundred times since coming to
Glasgow that had I but half the consecration to *my* business that I see in the lives of some businessmen to whom
I preach, I might be less haunted with the sense of doing
nothing. But that is by the way, my point is this—though
the minister does not understand, remember Christ does.
He can give advice to the most cunning fisherman, and
the fisherman will never regret that he adopted it. Con-
sult Him when all your labor is a failure. Go to Him on
the eve of every venture. Tell Him all about it. Ask His

advice on it. He knows far more about fishing than ever Peter did. It is such a pity that the fish should all be there, and that by a boat's breadth you should miss your share of them—the share which God in His providence meant for you, and which you lose because you will not take His way.

Wouldest Thou Be Made Whole?

G. Campbell Morgan (1863–1945) was the son of a British Baptist preacher and preached his first sermon when he was thirteen years old. He had no formal training for the ministry, but his tireless devotion to the study of the Bible helped him to become one of the leading Bible teachers of his day. Rejected by the Methodists, he was ordained into the Congregational ministry. He was associated with Dwight L. Moody in the Northfield Bible conferences and as an itinerant Bible teacher. He is best known as the pastor of the Westminster Chapel, London (1904–17 and 1933–45). During his second term there, he had Dr. D. Martyn Lloyd-Jones as his associate.

Morgan published more than sixty books and booklets, and his sermons are found in *The Westminster Pulpit* (London, Hodder and Stoughton, 1906–1916). This message was originally published in *The Northfield Echoes* and then in *The True Estimate of Life* (Fleming H. Revell, 1903).

G. Campbell Morgan

4

WOULDEST THOU BE MADE WHOLE?

Wilt thou be made whole? . . . Rise, take up thy bed, and walk. . . . sin no more, lest a worse thing come unto thee (John 5:6, 8, 14).

IT HAS BEEN very beautifully said that all the parables of Jesus are miracles of wisdom; that all the miracles of Jesus are parables of teaching. Believing that statement to be true, I propose here to consider this miracle of healing as a parable of teaching. In order that we may do this intelligently, suffer me to remind you again in a few words of the actual facts of the story from this fifth chapter of the gospel of John.

Jesus had come up to Jerusalem, and passing through the Bethesda porches, He had seen lying all around, a multitude of impotent folk, sick, and maimed, and halt, such as were in need of healing and of deliverance. But the one man who attracted His attention principally, was the one in all the crowd that most sorely needed help. Christ is always preeminently attracted by the most needy cases. This man had been in the grip of his infirmity for thirty-eight years.

Now, that is very easily said, but how very few of us can know its actual meaning. Thirty-eight years of helplessness, not strong enough now to be able to drag himself from the place where he lay in the porches into the pool, longing oftentimes to reach it, but always too late, some other having stepped down before him; and unable to persuade any man to help him day after day, week after week, month after month; and still, when Jesus passes through, he is impotent and needy; and in all likelihood, feebler and weaker than he had ever been.

Now, if you can for a moment, I pray you think of the surprise of the whole story. I feel that there is no more

47

dramatic incident in the New Testament than this. The crowds are thronging Jerusalem at the feast, the sick folk are lying all about in the porches at Bethesda, and undoubtedly a great multitude of people are passing, as Jesus passed, through those porches. As the Master comes, His eye rests upon this man, who lies there in all his need, and in all his weakness, and looking down at him, He says to him, "Wilt thou be made whole?"

And I can imagine with what astonishment the man looked up into the face of the Stranger; for I pray you remember the man did not know Him, did not know that it was the Prophet, mighty in deed and word, who was so strangely beginning to stir the whole country; and his very first word marks his astonishment—"Sir"—as though he had said, What do you mean by asking me a question like that?—"Sir, I have no man, when the water is troubled, to put me into the pool; but while I am coming, another steppeth down before me."

Then Jesus says, "Rise, take up thy bed, and walk," and I think I see a crowd gathering around. Human nature is just the same in every age. They begin to watch and wonder, and I think, if I had been in the crowd, I should have protested against what Jesus had said. I will tell you why presently. While the crowd gathers, the Christ quietly looks at the man, that man in the grip of an infirmity for thirty-eight years, so weak that he could not struggle his own way to the pool when the water was troubled, and he stands up, bends down again, picks up the bed upon which he had been lying, rolling it up in all probability, flings it on his shoulder, and walks, a whole man, out of the porches into which he had been carried.

And where is Jesus? He is gone. He conveyed Himself away; the crowd was coming after Him, and He departed.

Now the man starts his walk home, and some of the men who were far more eager about the observance of the Sabbath than the healing of an impotent man, stop him, and they say to him, "What right have you carrying your bed on the Sabbath?" And I like the man's answer, "The Man that healed me told me to do it." And they said, "Who is it that told you to do it?" You notice their question. They did not say, "Who is it that healed you?" They were so anxious about the Sabbath. Oh, these men that strain at gnats and swallow camels! "Who told you to carry your bed?" And he knew not that it was Jesus, and he told them he did not know, so there was an end of the strife.

Now, in all probability—if I can follow the story up, and I think I may do it correctly—he carried his bed home, and he put it down, and coming out of his house again, he made his way, eager and anxious to do what, perchance, he had not been able to do for long years, to mingle with the worshipers in the temple, back to the temple courts, back to the songs of Zion, back to worship. And as he is there among the worshipers, moving around, perchance greeting old friends, to their utter astonishment, suddenly he stands again face-to-face with the Man who healed him. Jesus is in front of him. And Jesus looks into his face as he stands erect, and He says to him, "Behold, thou art made whole; sin no more, lest a worse thing come unto thee." And again the Master passes away; and so far as we know, did not speak to the man again.

But in those three things that Jesus said to him, I have a radiant revelation of His perpetual method of dealing with man. First He arrested his attention, called his mind into play, and appealed to his will, "Wouldest thou be made whole?" And then He called him to act, to put into action the new consciousness and passion that had taken possession of his soul, "Arise, take up thy bed, and walk." And then, after he was healed, He conditioned all his life for him in a very simple law. He pronounced him whole, "Thou art made whole"; and then He laid a commandment on him, "Sin no more"; and then He lit for him a solemn and suggestive lamp of warning, "lest a worse thing come unto thee."

Now, shall we take these three stages in the Master's method and attempt to look at them a little more closely.

Wilt Thou Be Made Whole?

Take the first, "Wilt thou be made whole?" The question is so simple that it seems as though we might dismiss it, and say nothing about it; and yet I am sure that that would be a great mistake, because the question that appears so simple is indeed sublime.

There are at least four facts within the compass of that question that we are bound to examine, if we would understand Christ's method with men.

First, the Lord Jesus recognizes the royalty of human will. Do you want to be made whole? And I say it very reverently at once, unless he does Christ can do nothing for him. But there is more than that in the question. There is, not apparent in the question, but quite evident from what followed it, a revelation to the man of his degradation. You want to be made whole? And immediately the man's question reveals the fact that he never expected to be made whole, that he had lost heart, that he had lost hope. He said, "Sir, I have no man, when the water is troubled, to put me into the pool; but while I am coming, another steppeth down before me"; which, being translated into other words, means this, It is no use asking me such a question, I have not any chance of being made whole. He had lost hope, and Christ's question revealed the fact.

And yet is there not in the question of Christ, because Christ asks it, a renewal of the very hope he had lost? The fact that the man answered him at all shows that suddenly there was springing up in the man's heart the hope that was dead. Why did he answer Christ?

No, no, ask another question; ask the question that in all probability the man asked, as he lay there, "What made this Man say that to me? Whole! did He say? Why, there is the song of birds in the very word, and the breath of summer seems round about me once again. Whole? What does He mean? Is He going to do something for me? Is this the Man I have been waiting for, that will help me when no one else can?" And I think that while there is evidently a revelation of the degradation of the man, in that he had lost hope, there is also a revelation of the fact that the question renewed his hope.

And yet once again, not only the recognition of royalty of will, and the revelation of degradation, and the renewal of hope, but surely a requirement, a claim upon the man suggested, in order to the end that is desired; the arrest of the man, that the man may be ready for something else. If Christ stands outside that man's will, and asks that it may consent; and if Christ, standing outside the man, reveals the man's degradation; and if, in the very question, He renews his hope; is there not a hint, an inference, a suggestion, that if he is going to have any wholeness that Christ can give him he must be ready to do what Christ tells him? So that, it seems to me, we have at least four things revealed in this question. When Christ comes to deal with a man that is impotent, a man that is in the grip of some mastering disease that is sapping his life and spoiling his days, first He recognizes the royalty of human will; secondly, He reveals the fact of degradation, that hope is lost; thirdly, He renews hope by the very fact of His coming, and His question; and lastly, He requires submission to whatever He shall say, if the benefit that He is ready and willing to confer is to be obtained.

Now, for the moment, let us pass from the story, and attempt to apply this revelation of its meaning to ourselves. If this study has any value in it, it has that value as we are conscious of our sin, conscious of our shortcomings, conscious that we are not what we would be, conscious of the passions that master us, of the evil things that hold us in their grip. If Christ is indeed to heal spiritually; if men are to lose the chains that bind them; if indeed "the pulses of desire" are to feel the touch of "His coolness and balm"; if the poison that has burned in our veins like a veritable fever is to be quenched; there are certain things that we have to look solemnly in the face, things that are suggested by this very first question.

Jesus confronts you, my brother, my sister, personally, individually, in loneliness; and the question He is now asking you is this: Do you want to be made whole?

Now, let me say at once to you, if you do not, then I have no message for you further. I think we may just as well take these things step-by-step, and be quite serious about them, and businesslike about them. If there is a man who has no desire to be made whole, no desire after pureness, no desire after wholeness, no desire after a higher mode of life, no desire after the things that are beautiful, the things that are of good report, then I have no further message for that man. You drop out of my argument, you drop out of my message; I have nothing more to say to you. I have no warrant to deliver any evangel of power and of blessing to the man that does not want to be made whole.

But now, hear me. Is there such a man? There may be, but I very much doubt it. I wonder if that statement sounds at all astonishing. I will repeat it, as revealing a growing conviction in my heart and life, as I work for God, that you will have a very great difficulty in finding me the man that does not want to be made whole. Oh, but you say, look at the men who are sinning, and sinning with a high hand and outstretched arm. Look at the men that have all kinds of chances of amendment. Look at the men who have heard the Gospel message from childhood up, and yet are sinning on. Do you mean to tell us, someone is saying, that you think those men really want to be made whole? In a vast majority of cases I believe they do.

I remember one early morning as far back as the year 1887. I had been out all through the night, sitting by the bedside of a dying man in the town of Hull in the north of England, and as I was taking my way home, having seen him pass away, about four o'clock in the morning, turning suddenly around a corner, I came face-to-face with a young fellow, the son of godly people, a child of tender care and constant prayer, and yet who, having fallen, was just going all the pace in wickedness; and meeting him suddenly like that, just turning the corner so that there was no escape, he and I stood face-to-face. He was hurrying home through the gray morning after a night of carousal. I took his hand in mine, and I looked into his face, and I said, "Charley, when are you going to stop this kind of thing?"

I wish I could tell what that man said, and how he said it. I shall never forget it, I think, to my dying day. He looked into my face, a young man just about my own age at the time, and yet prematurely aged, with sunken cheek and bloodshot eye, and that gray ashen hue that tells of debauchery; and holding out a hand that he could not hold still, that trembled as he held it, he said, "What do you mean by asking me when I am going to stop?" He said, "I would lose that hand here and now, if I knew how to stop." I do not think that was a lonely case. I believe that if you could only get hold of half these men that are going wrong, if you could only get hold of them, and press them up into some corner in the early morning, catching them unawares, when they are not prepared to debate the thing with you or laugh at your entreaty, they would speak out a great truth, and it would be—we want to be pure, we hate impurity.

Oh, I know you will suggest a hundred whys. Oh, yes, I know all the whys, but face the fact first. I very much doubt if you can find me a young fellow who is playing the fool with himself, and sinning, sinning, sinning, but that if you could get back of the exterior, if you could only know what is going on in his own heart, you would find a man who wants to be made whole. Profoundly do I believe it.

Now, Christ asks first, that if that is true, if I am right about you, that you will say so to Him now. That is His first question.

But now, take the next step. This man did want to be made whole. The question seems to be superfluous in one sense. I can imagine that the man might have said to Jesus, What makes You ask me that? Do You suppose I love lying here? Do You suppose I am fond of this infirmity? Do You suppose that I really am delighted with this spoilation of my life? The man did not say all that. What then did he say? He said the next thing. He said in effect, Sir, it is no use to ask me, I cannot be made whole. I tried, but I never got down to the troubled water. I have been waiting for a man to help me; that man has never come. It is no good, do not ask me about being whole. Of course I want to be whole, but I never shall.

Now here we are touching the reason why so many of these men are continuing in sin. They have lost heart, they have lost hope, they do not believe they can mend. When, every now and then, one of them comes to talk to me, or to some Christian worker, and the whole truth is talked out in straightness, that is the story we have to hear again and again. A man says to us, Oh, I would give anything if I could go right, but I cannot; it is no good. I have tried and tried and tried, and failed and failed and failed. I have been to meetings, and I have been to ministers, and I have been to all sorts of people, and I have never yet been able to stand up and be strong, since I became the slave of sin. A man comes to me and says, I am in the grip of a passion for drink. Oh, the number of such men that one has to deal with. And he says, I want to go right, God knows I want to go right, but I cannot.

Said a man to me some years ago, who was a member of my congregation, a man of splendid parts, a man who, every now and then, just broke out and simply went mad with drink; and I went to see him as he was getting back out of one of these terrible drinking bouts, and sitting in his house with him, he looked at me with a sort of disdain in his face, the disdain which is the mark, not of unkindness, but of inward agony; and he said, "Mr. Morgan, what is the good of your talking to me? You don't know anything about this passion for drink, you don't know what it means." Said he, "When the thirst is on me, if you put a glass of wine on that table, and standing on the other side of it, you told me that if I touched it you would shoot me, and I knew that hell lay the other side of the bullet, I would drink that wine."

Now, don't you people that know nothing about it think that that is fanaticism. There is many a man in that condition. The grip of sin in the form of a passion for drink is awful. When it gets hold of a man it becomes more than a spiritual sin, it becomes more than a mental aberration, it becomes a physical disease. Many a man is in that condition, and he will tell you he has tried and tried, and failed and failed. Doesn't that man want to be right? Of course he does. What, then, is the matter with him? He has lost hope; he has lost heart. He is saying exactly what this man said, There is nobody can help me; don't talk to me about being whole.

But what next? And oh, my brother, I am talking to

you. God knows just what you are doing, nursing your agony, hiding your sin, hidden in the world from everybody except the Master.

Now, may I not say to you this, that just as the question of Jesus suggested to this man another possibility, very faint, very unlikely, and yet, perchance, something in it; and just as the question of Jesus brought to this man a new hope—may I not say to you now that the question of Christ ought to, and I believe is, bringing a new hope into your life? You know I want to take you just where you are, my brother, and help you. I want to take you right down there in the midst of your weakness, I want to take you with that underlying passion for wholeness, and that overlying conception that you can't have it, and I want to say to you, isn't the very fact that you are willing to listen, and that God's message is being delivered to you, and that once again the question of the Christ is coming to you personally, Do you want to be made whole?—is not there something in it at least that ought to suggest to you that there is half a chance, if no more, that Christ may be able to do something for you?

Oh, I will take you on your half chance, if you will only come, because my Master did. I like to see the men that came to Him, not quite sure that they would get anything, and they always got what they wanted. There was a man one day came to Him, and said to Him, If Thou canst do anything for my boy. It was a poor faith, it was a faith that came on a crutch—"If Thou canst." And did Jesus say to him, Well, if that is all your confidence, you had better go away; if you question My power, I have nothing for you? No, no, Christ never does that kind of thing. If a man cannot come without his "if" Christ will bless him, notwithstanding his "if," if he will come. Christ flung the "if" back at him, and He said, "If thou canst believe, all things are possible," and he got his blessing.

And there was another man came to Christ, a good deal meaner than that one. This man that came to Christ did not say, "If Thou canst." We have little respect for that man. But the other man said, "If Thou wilt." He did not question the power so much as the willingness. And was Jesus offended, and did He send him away because he came with an "if"? No, oh no. He gave him His blessing. He said, Do you doubt My willingness? Listen. "I will; be thou clean," and the man was clean. So that if you are coming upon a crutch tonight, come. If you are coming tonight, saying as you come, I don't think there is much in this, we have heard this kind of thing before; if you are saying, as many a man has said to me, Oh, I have been out in the after-meeting before, never mind, come on the half chance. Take your half chance. That is what Christ has come to do now, just to give you a gleam of light. Oh, a great deal more than that; but that is the first thing, and if you want to be made whole, I tell you, man, the fact that you are seeking light is a sign, or ought to be a sign to you, that there may be a chance even for you.

Now, follow to the last of these points, the royalty of will, the revelation of degradation, the renewal of hope, and the requirement of submission. Let me talk now as out of the experience of the man himself who lies in the porch. He asks me if I want to be made whole? Of course I do. He asks me if I want to be made whole? What is the use, I can't. He asks me if I want to be made whole? He must mean something; surely He means something. I am inclined to think He means something. If so, I shall have to do whatever He says. Ah, that is it. That is the last thing.

The question must come to that point. It is a wonderful question, one of Christ's questions, recognizing the man's royalty of will, standing outside him until he wants Him, and then flashing upon him his own degradation, and making him say there was no chance, and yet kindling in his heart the new passion for wholeness; and then suggesting, so that the man cannot escape the suggestion, that if this Stranger was going to do anything for him, then he must be willing to do what the Stranger should tell him to do. So far it is all mental.

Rise, Take Up Thy Bed, and Walk

What is the next thing? Now Christ passes from the realm of the mind into the realm of action, and He says to him three things altogether, "Rise, take up thy bed, and walk." I do not want to insult your intelligence, and yet I want you to remember He does not say, "Walk, take up thy bed, and arise." Get right hold of that. That is what some of you are trying to do. You are trying to walk before you are up. You can't do it! He began with the first thing, and then the second thing, and then the third thing. "Arise, take up thy bed"—some of you would have left out the middle of it; some of you would have said, Arise and walk; oh no, the value of it you will see presently—"Rise, take up thy bed, and walk."

Now, what is the first thing a man has to do if he is going to be made whole? First, "Arise." But what is this? What is the rising that this man is called to do? I pray you notice very carefully what this is. It is the one thing that he can't do that Christ tells him to do first. That is what made me say at the beginning of the sermon that if I had been in that crowd, I think I would have protested.

Let us go back, and imagine we are there. The porches, the sick folk, this worst case of all. A Stranger coming through suddenly stops and says, Do you want to be made whole? and the man says, It is no use, I can't get into the water, there is nobody to put me in. And then the Stranger says "Arise!" Why, my dear sir, I should feel inclined to say to Him, This is absurd; this is the one thing the man can't do. What do you suppose he is lying here for all these years, if he could get up? Of course he can't arise. I am prepared to say to this Stranger, first, it is impossible, and therefore it is unreasonable; and I am not going to change these decisions. Impossible, and unreasonable, and I utter my protest.

Why, what is this! The man is up! The man is up while I am arguing! Was I wrong to say it was impossible? Certainly not. Was I wrong to say it was unreasonable? Certainly not. But he is up. I know it, but he has done the impossible and the unreasonable thing.

That is the miracle of Christianity. That is the revelation of Christ's perpetual method with a man He is going to heal. Are you in the grip of some evil passion, of some evil habit? For I call you to notice that sin in every man focuses itself at some one point preeminently, and you know that you would have been in the kingdom of God years ago, but for one thing. You know what the one thing is, and when Christ begins to deal with you, He brings you face-to-face with your impossibility, and He says, "Now, begin there!"

To the young man who was a ruler, and wealthy, Jesus said, "One thing thou lackest." What was the one thing he lacked? Some men would have said it was poverty. But these are the men who do not read their Bible carefully. What was it he lacked? Control! "Follow Me." But what was the hindrance between his life of self-control and his life of being controlled by another? What lay between? His wealth. Now, Christ said, Sell that, give that up, put that away. There was nothing more impossible in all that man's life than that he should part with his wealth, and He brought him face-to-face with his impossibility.

There was a man in the synagogue one day whom Jesus called out, and he came and stood in front. What is the matter with that man? A withered hand! What will Christ tell him to do, to hold his other hand up? No, certainly not. What then? To hold out the withered hand! the one he can't hold out. He always brings the man face-to-face with the impossible thing. Always this, always this—the impossible thing!

My dear sir, Christ is not going to ask *you* to give up the drink. Certainly not. Why not? Because it is not your impossible thing. He is not going to ask you, my dear sir, to sign a pledge against swearing. Why not? Because you never do it. That is the human method. The human method is to get one, or two, or three little pledges, and try to make them fit everybody. And oh, how eager men are to give up their brothers' idols!

Oh, the difficulty of it, and yet the magnificence of it! Christ is dealing with every man alone just now, and you know what He is saying to you at your weakest point: Begin and do the right thing. Arise!

But now I say, while I am arguing, the man has done it, and you may do it. Shall we try and find out how this man did it? This is the great secret. There is no problem of such interest as to know how that man got up when he could not get up. I will tell you exactly how it happened, and I will tell you because I know, experimentally and personally, how it happened.

Let us look at it. Christ first addressed his will—Wilt thou? That is the first thing. When Christ says "Arise!" it means that His will is that the man should be made whole. Now, mark another thing. There is power enough in Christ to make him whole. Christ is quite equal to supply him with all he needs. There is, however, only one way in which there can be connection made between the power of Christ and the impotence of the man. The man cannot; Christ can. How are you going to get together the man's cannot and Christ's can? That is what we want to find out. When Christ said "Arise," the man said to himself, I want to be made whole, but it's no good, yet I wonder what this Man means. I will do what He says. I cannot, but I will, because He says so.

Now mark, Christ's will and the man's will touch, and in that connection, the connection of will with will, the power of the Christ flashes into the man, and he stands erect, not in the energy of will, but in the energy of Christ, which has become his, because he has submitted his will to the will of the Christ.

That is the way you are going to master that evil thing in your life, my brother, or you will never master it. It is the Christ power that you need to set you on your feet and make you live. And you can only come into connection with the Christ power when you will to do what He tells you to do. Oh, but you say, I cannot. As long as you say that, you will not. But supposing you try another way. Say no longer "I will," you have said that scores of times, and been beaten. Do not say "I cannot," for as long as you say that you never will.

What, then, shall you say? Say this, "I cannot, but because He said so I will!" You see in that there is an abandonment to Him, you are handing your life over to Him, you do it in obedience to Him; and whenever a man takes that stand, all the power he needs for the breaking of the chains that bind him are at his disposal, and he will stand up erect, able to do the impossible, doing by faith the unreasonable, because his abandonment of will and his act of faith have brought him into living contact with the Christ of God.

And now the man is up, what next? "Take up thy bed, and walk." Take up thy bed! I think one of the most illuminative and most beautiful things I have ever seen about that is from the pen of Dr. Marcus Dods, just in a sentence and a flash. Dr. Dods says, "Why was the man to take up his bed? In order that there should be no provision made for a relapse." Ah, that is the point. Did you hear that? I don't want you to miss that. No provision for a relapse. That is the principle upon which a man is to start his Christian life.

The temptation to this man was to say, Well, I am up; I am up, really I am; yes, really I am up, and He has done it; but I think I'd better leave that bed; I don't know how I will get on in the street; I don't know how I will get on tomorrow; I'd better leave it, in case I have to come back. As sure as he had done it, he would have come back. Oh, no, no, that won't do! Jesus says, Take you, master the thing that has mastered you; take it up! take it up!

May I put the principle in other words, and declare it thus, When you start to follow Christ, burn your bridges behind you! Don't give yourself a chance to go back. I do not think too much emphasis can be laid upon that. Oh, the men that leave the bridge, and presently slip back over it!

Here is a man who has been, to revert to my previous illustration, the slave of drink; he says, "Now, I am going to quit this in the strength of Christ," and my profound conviction is that is the only way a man can quit. "I am going to do it." He means it, and he gets up and starts; when he gets home, in some cupboard in his house is a half bottle of whiskey. What is he going to do with it? Oh, he says, I will drive the cork right in, and I will put a seal on it, and I won't touch it, and I will keep it in case I am in need of it. I tell you, that man will want whiskey within twenty-four hours.

No, no! If that has been your besetment, when you get home, smash it, pour it out! I am not going to say soft, easy things. I am not going to tell you all you have to do is to believe. I want to tell you that you are to believe with the belief that manifests itself in works, and unless you have a belief like that, it is worth nothing. Burn your bridges, cut off your companionships, and say farewell to the men that have been luring you to ruin. Be a man, stand up, and say to the man that tempted you, and drew you aside, your dearest friend, "I have done, I have done; I am going the other way." And I want to say this to you, the chances are all in favor of the fact that the man will come with you. That is the remarkable thing about it, that the very man that is luring you to wrong will very likely come with you, if you are only man enough to burn your bridges. Take up your bed and walk.

"And walk!" I would like to tell you all there is in that. I will tell you one thing that is in it. Don't expect to be carried! I want to tell you that the churches are altogether too full of perambulator Christians—men and women who have to be nursed and coddled by the ministers to keep them there at all; men and women who say, "If you don't call, then I am going." Oh, go! Give us a chance!

Now, if you are going to start to follow Christ, young man, young woman, my brother, my sister, WALK. And remember, that when He gives you power to stand up, He gives you power to carry your bed, after you walk—a great sufficiency of power.

Then Jesus met this man once again. What did He say to him then? "Thou art made whole!" Has He ever said that to you? No, some one says, I don't think He has. Then you are not a Christian. Don't be satisfied because someone else said you are made whole. Never rest until He has said it to your inmost soul, and you know it.

Sin No More, Lest a Worse Thing Come unto Thee

But when He does say it, then what? "Sin no more." Now have done with your argument as to whether you are compelled to sin or not. He says "no." How dare you,

child of His love, child of His blood, child of His power—
how dare you go on sinning, and say you can't help it,
when He looks you in the face, and says, "Sin no more!"
He never says that to a man until He has made him
whole. He does not begin by saying that. He does not go to
the man that is impotent, to the man that is weak, He
does not say tonight to the man that is outside the kingdom, "Sin no more." He first heals him, He first gives him
power, and then He tells him to "sin no more."

What else does He say? He says this, "lest a worse
thing come unto thee." What could be worse? To go back
to your impotence, to go back to the old disease, and have
no one come and heal you. That could be worse.

I leave you to follow the lines of that indefinite and
solemn warning that Christ uttered to the man, but I
pray you remember it. If you have been healed, if you
have been made whole, if you have been born again, and
you are playing with sin, and sinning on, excusing it as
an infirmity, remember Christ's word comes tonight, swift,
scorching, scathing—"Sin no more, lest a worse thing come
unto thee."

Where is my last word to be uttered? Back in the middle
of the story. "Arise," says the Master, make a beginning,
make a start, and make your start, not by making up
your mind that you are going to do great things, but by
making up your mind that Christ is going to do great
things, and you are going to let Him. That is the very
heart of the message! That is the secret of power!

NOTES

The Gradual Healing of the Blind Man

Alexander Maclaren (1826–1910) was one of Great Britain's most famous preachers. While pastoring the Union Chapel, Manchester (1858–1903), he became known as "the prince of expository preachers." Rarely active in denominational or civic affairs, Maclaren invested his time in studying the Word in the original and sharing its truths with others in sermons that are still models of effective expository preaching. He published a number of books of sermons and climaxed his ministry by publishing his monumental *Expositions of Holy Scripture*.

This message is taken from *A Year's Ministry*, published by Funk and Wagnalls Company (1902).

Alexander Maclaren

5

THE GRADUAL HEALING OF THE BLIND MAN

And [Jesus] cometh to Bethsaida; and they bring a blind man unto him, and besought him to touch him. And he took the blind man by the hand, and led him out of the town; and when he had spit on his eyes, and put his hands upon him, he asked him if he saw ought. And he looked up, and said, I see men as trees, walking. After that he put his hands again upon his eyes and made him look up: and he was restored and saw every man clearly (Mark 8:22–25).

THIS MIRACLE, which is only recorded by the Evangelist Mark, has about it several very peculiar features. Some of these it shares with one other of our Lord's miracles, which also is found only in this gospel, and which occurred about the same time; that miracle of healing the deaf and dumb man recorded in the previous chapter. Both of them have these points in common: that our Lord takes the sufferer away and works His miracle in privacy; that in both there is an abundant use of the same singular means—our Lord's touch, and the saliva upon His finger; and that in both there is the urgent injunction of entire secrecy laid upon the recipient of the benefit.

But this miracle had another peculiarity, in which it stands absolutely alone, and that is that the work is done in stages; that the power which at other times has but to speak and it is done, here seems to labor, and the cure comes slowly; that in the middle Christ pauses, and like a physician trying the experiment of a drug, asks the patient if any effect is produced, and getting the answer that some mitigation is realized, repeats the application, and perfect recovery is the result.

Now, how unlike that is to all the rest of Christ's miraculous working we do not need to point out; but the question may arise, what is the meaning, and what the reason, and what the lessons of this unique and anomalous form of miraculous working? It is to that question that I wish to turn now: for I think that the answer will open up to us some very precious things in regard to that great Lord, the revelation of whose heart and character is the inmost and the loftiest meaning both of His words and of His works.

I take these three points of peculiarity to which I have referred: the privacy, the strange and abundant use of means veiling the miraculous power, and the gradual, slow nature of the cure. I see in them these three things: Christ isolating the man that He would heal; Christ stooping to the sense-bound nature by using outward means; and Christ making His power work slowly, to keep abreast of the man's slow faith.

Christ Isolates the Man Whom He Wanted to Heal

First, then, here we have Christ isolating the man whom He wanted to heal. Now, there may have been something about our Lord's circumstances and purposes at the time of this miracle which accounted for the great urgency with which at this period He impresses secrecy upon all around Him. What that was it is not necessary for us to inquire here, but this is worth noticing, that in obedience to this wish, on His own part, for privacy at the time, He covers over with a veil His miraculous working, and does it quietly, as one might almost say, in a corner. He never sought to display His miraculous working; here He absolutely tries to hide it. That fact of Christ taking pains to conceal His miracle carries in it two great truths: first, about the purpose and nature of miracles in general, and second, about His character, as to each of which a few words may be said.

This fact, of a miracle done in intended secrecy, and shrouded in deep darkness, suggests to us the true point of view from which to look at the whole subject of miracles.

People say they were meant to be attestations of His Divine mission. Yes, no doubt that is true partially; but that was never the sole nor even the main purpose for which they were wrought; and when anybody asked Jesus

Christ to work a miracle for that purpose only, He rebuked the desire and refused to gratify it. He wrought the miracle, not coldly, in order to witness to His mission, but every one of them was the token, because it was the outcome, of His own sympathetic heart, brought into contact with human need. And instead of the miracles of Jesus Christ being cold, logical proofs of His mission, they were all glowing with the earnestness of a loving sympathy, and came from Him at sight of sorrow as naturally as rays from the sun.

Then, on the other hand, the same fact carries with it, too, a lesson about His character. Is not He here doing what He tells us to do; "Let not thy left hand know what thy right hand doeth"? He dares not wrap His talent in a napkin, He would be unfaithful to His mission if He hid His light under a bushel. All goodness "does good by stealth," even if it does not "blush to find it fame"—and that universal mark of true benevolence marked His. He had to solve in His human life what we have to solve, the problem of keeping the narrow path between ostentation of powers and selfish concealment of faculty; and He solved it thus, leaving us an example that we should follow in His steps.

But that is somewhat aside from the main purpose to which I wanted to turn in these first remarks. Christ did not invest the miracle with any of its peculiarities for His own sake only. All that is singular about it, will, I think, find its best explanation in the condition and character of the subject, the man on whom it was wrought. What sort of a man was he? Well, the narrative does not tell us much, but if we use our historical imagination and our eyes we may learn something about him. First he was a Gentile; the land in which the miracle was wrought was the half-heathen country on the east side of the Sea of Galilee. In the second place, it was other people that brought him; he does not come of his own accord. Then again, it is their prayer that is mentioned, not his—he asks nothing.

You see him standing there, hopeless, listless; not believing that this Jewish stranger is going to do anything for him; with his impassive blind face glowing with no entreaty to reinforce his companions' prayers. And suppose he is a man of that sort, with no expectation of anything from this rabbi, how is Christ to get at him? It is no use talking to him. His eyes are shut, so cannot see the sympathy beaming in His face. There is one thing possible—to lay hold of Him by the hand; and the touch, gentle, loving, firm, says this, at least: "Here is a man that has some interest in me, and whether He can do anything or not for me, He is going to try something." Would not that kindle an expectation in him? And is it not in parable just exactly what Jesus Christ does for the whole world? Is not that act of His by which He put out His hand and seized the unbelieving limp hand of the blind man that hung by his side, the very same in principle as that by which He "taketh hold of the seed of Abraham," and is made like to His brethren? Is not the mystery of the Incarnation and the meaning of it wrapped up as in a germ in that little simple incident, He put out His hand and touched him?

Is there not in it too a lesson for all you good-hearted Christian men and women, in all your work? If you want to do anything for your Master and for your brethren, there is only one way to do it—to come down to their level and get hold of their hands, and then there is some chance of doing them good. We must be content to take the hands of beggars if we are to make the blind to see.

And then, having thus drawn near to the man, and established in his heart some dim expectation of something coming, He gently draws him away out of the little village. I wonder no painter has ever painted that, instead of repeating *ad nauseam* two or three scenes out of the Gospels. I wonder none of them has ever seen what a parable it is—the Christ leading the blind man out into solitude before He can say to him "Behold!" How as they went, step-by-step, the poor blind eyes not telling the man where they were going, or how far away he was being taken from his friends, his conscious dependence upon this Stranger would grow! How he would feel more and more at each step, "I am at His mercy! What *is* He going to do with me?" And how thus there would be kindled in his heart some beginnings of an expectation, as well as some surrendering of himself to Christ's guidance! These two things, the expectation and the surrender, have in them at all events some faint beginnings and rude germs of the highest faith, to lead up to which is the purpose of all that Christ here does.

And is not that what He does for us all? Sometimes by sorrows, sometimes by sickbeds, sometimes by shutting us out from chosen spheres of activity, sometimes by striking down the dear ones at our sides, and leaving us lonely in the desert—is He not saying to us in a thousand ways. "Come ye yourselves apart into a desert place"? As Israel was led into the wilderness that God might "speak to her heart," so often Christ draws us aside, if not by outward providences such as these, yet by awaking in us that solemn sense of personal responsibility and making us feel our solitude, that He may lead us to feel His all-sufficient companionship.

Ah! brethren, here is a lesson from all this—if you want Jesus Christ to give you His highest gifts and to reveal to you His fairest beauty, you must be alone with Him. He loves to deal with single souls. Our lives, many of them, can never be outwardly alone. We are jammed up against one another in such a fashion, and the hurry and pressure of city life is so great with us all that it is often impossible for us to find the outward secrecy and solitude. But a man may be alone in a crowd; the heart may be gathered up into itself, and there may be a still atmosphere round about us in the shop and in the market, and among the busy ways of men, in which we and Christ shall be alone together. Unless there be, I do not think any of us will see the King in His beauty or the far-off land. "I was left alone, and saw this great vision" is the law for all true beholding.

So, dear brethren, try to feel how awful this earthly life of ours is in its necessary solitude; that each of us by himself must shape out his own destiny, and make his own character; that every unit of the swarms upon our streets is a unit that has to face the solemn facts of life for and by itself that alone you live, that alone you will die;

that alone you will have to give account of yourself before God, and in the solitude let the hand of your heart feel for His hand that is stretched out to grasp yours, and listen to Him saying "Lo, I am with you always even unto the end of the world." There was no dreariness in the solitude when it was *Christ* that "took the blind man by the hand, and led him out of the town."

Christ Stooping to a Sense-Bound Nature by the Use of Material Helps

Second, we have Christ stooping to a sense-bound nature by the use of material helps. No doubt there was something in the man, as I have said, which made it advisable that these methods should be adopted. If he were the sort of person that I have described, slow of faith, not much caring about the possibility of cure, and not having much hope that anything would come of it—then we can see the fitness of the means adopted; the hand laid upon the eyes, the finger possibly moistened with saliva touching the ball, the pausing to question, the repeated application. They make a ladder by which his hope and confidence might climb to the apprehension of the blessing. And that points to a general principle of the Divine dealings. God stoops to a feeble faith, and gives to it outward things by which it may rise to an apprehension of spiritual realities.

Is not that the meaning of the whole complicated system of Old Testament revelation? Is not that the meaning of the altars, and priests, and sacrifices, and the old cumbrous apparatus of the Mosaic law? Was it not all a picture book in which the infant eyes of the race might see in a material form deep spiritual realities? Was not that the meaning and explanation of our Lord's parabolic teaching? He veils spiritual truth in common things that He may reveal it by common things—taking fishermen's boats, their nets, a sower's basket, a baker's dough, and many another homely article, and finding in them the emblems of the loftiest truth.

Is not that the meaning of His own Incarnation? It is no use talking to men about God, let them see Him; no use preaching about principles, give them the facts of His life. Revelation does not consist in the setting forth of certain propositions about God, but in the exhibition of the acts of God in a human life.

> And so the Word was flesh and wrought
> With human hands the creed of creeds.

And still further, may we not say that this is the inmost meaning and purpose of the whole frame of the material universe? It exists in order that, as a parable and a symbol, it may proclaim the things that are unseen and eternal. Its depths and heights, its splendors, and its energies are all in order that through them spirits may climb to the apprehension of the "King eternal, immortal, invisible," and the realities of His spiritual kingdom.

So in regard of all the externals of Christianity, forms of worship, ordinances, and so on—all these, in like manner, are provided in condescension to our weakness, in order that by them we may be lifted above themselves; for the purpose of the temple is to prepare for the time and the place where the seer "saw no temple therein." They are but the cups that carry the wine, the flowers whose chalices bear the honey, the ladders by which the soul may climb to God Himself, the rafts upon which the precious treasure may be floated into our hearts.

If Christ's touch and Christ's saliva healed, it was not because of anything in them, but because He willed it so and He Himself is the source of all the healing energy. Therefore, let us keep these externals in their proper place of subordination, and remember that in Him, not in them, lies the healing power; and that even Christ's touch may become the object of superstitious regard, as it was when that poor woman that came through the crowd to lay her finger on the hem of His garment, thinking that she could bear away a surreptitious blessing without the conscious outgoing of His power. He healed her because there was a spark of faith in her superstition, but she had to learn that it was not the hem of the garment but the loving will of Christ that cured, in order that the dross of superstitious reliance on the outward vehicle might be melted away, and the pure gold of faith in His love and power might remain.

Christ Accommodating the Pace of His Power to the Slowness of the Man's Faith

Lastly, we have Christ accommodating the pace of His power to the slowness of the man's faith. The whole story, as I have said, is unique, and especially that part of it—"He put his hands upon him, and asked him if he saw ought." One might have expected an answer with a little more gratitude in it, with a little more wonder in it, with a little more emotion in it. Instead of these it is almost surly, or at any rate strangely reticent—a matter-of-fact answer to the question, and there an end. As our Revised Version reads it better: "I see men, for I behold them as trees walking." Curiously accurate! A dim glimmer had come into the eye, but there is not yet distinctness of outline nor sense of magnitude, which must be acquired by practice. The eye has not yet been educated, and it was only because these blurred figures were in motion that he knew they were not trees. "After that he put his hands again upon his eyes and made him look up." Or as the Revised Version has it with a better reading, "and he looked stedfastly." An eager straining of the new faculty to make sure that he had got it, and to test its limits and its perfection. "And he was restored and saw all things clearly."

Now I take it that the worthiest view of that strangely protracted process, broken up into two halves by the question that is dropped into the middle, is this, that it was determined by the man's faith, and was meant to increase it. He was healed slowly because he believed slowly. His faith was a condition of his cure, and the measure of it determined the measure of the restoration and the rate of the growth of his faith settled the rate of the perfecting of Christ's work on him. As a rule, faith in His power to heal was a condition of Christ's healing, and that mainly because our Lord would rather have men believing than sound of body. They often wanted only the outward miracle, but He wanted to make it the means of insinuating a better healing into their spirits. And so, not that there was any necessary connection between their faith and the exercise of His miraculous power, but in order that He might bless them with His best gifts, He usually worked on the principle, "According to your faith be it unto you." And here, as a nurse or a mother with her child might do, He keeps step with the little steps, and goes slowly because the man goes slowly.

Now, both the gradual process of illumination and the rate of that process as determined by faith, are true for us. How dim and partial a glimmer of light comes to many a soul at the outset of the Christian life! How little a new convert knows about God and self and the starry truths of His great revelation! Christian progress does not consist in seeing new things, but in seeing the old thing more clearly: the same Christ, the same Cross, only more distinctly and deeply apprehended, and more closely incorporated into my very being. We do not grow away from Him, but we grow into knowledge of Him. The first lesson that we get is the last lesson that we shall learn, and He is the Alpha at the beginning, and the Omega at the end of the alphabet—the letters of which make up our knowledge for earth and heaven.

But then let me remind you that just in the measure in which you expect blessing of any kind, illumination and purifying and help of all sorts from Jesus Christ, just in that measure will you get it. You can limit the working of Almighty power, and can determine the rate at which it shall work on you. God fills the waterpots to the brim, but not beyond the brim; and if, like the woman in the Old Testament story, we stop bringing vessels, the oil will stop flowing. It is an awful thing to think that we have the power, as it were, to turn a stopcock, and so increase or diminish, or cut off altogether the supply of God's mercy and Christ's healing and cleansing love in our hearts. You will get as much of God as you want and no more. The measure of your desire is the measure of your capacity, and the measure of your capacity is the measure of God's gift. "Open thy mouth wide and I will fill it." And if your faith is heavily shod and steps slowly, His power and His grace will step slowly along with it; keeping rank and step. According to your faith shall it be unto you.

Ah, dear friends, desire Him to help and bless you, and He will do it. Expect Him to do it, and He will do it. Go to Him like the other blind man, and say to Him—"Jesus, Thou Son of David, have mercy on me . . . that I might receive my sight," and He will lay His hand upon you, and at any rate a glimmer will come, which will grow in the measure of your humble, confident desire, until at last He takes you by the hand and leads you out of this poor little village of a world, and lays His finger for a brief moment of blindness upon your eyes and asks you if you see ought. Then you look up, and the first face that you behold shall be His, whom you saw as "through a glass, darkly" with your dim eyes in this twilight world.

May that be your experience and mine, through His mercy!

NOTES

Malchus—The Last Miracle

Clarence Edward Macartney (1879–1957) ministered in Paterson, New Jersey, and Philadelphia, Pennsylvania, before assuming the influential pastorate of First Presbyterian Church, Pittsburgh, Pennsylvania, where he ministered for twenty-seven years. His preaching especially attracted men, not only to the Sunday services but also to his popular Tuesday noon luncheons. He was gifted in dealing with Bible biographies, and, in this respect, has well been called "the American Alexander Whyte." Much of his preaching was topical-textual, but it was always biblical, doctrinal, and practical. Perhaps his most famous sermon is "Come Before Winter."

The sermon I have selected is taken from *The Woman of Tekoah*, copyright renewed 1984 by the American Tract Society, published in 1955 by Abingdon Press, and included here by permission of the publisher.

Clarence Edward Macartney

6

MALCHUS—THE LAST MIRACLE

And he touched his ear, and healed him (Luke 22:51).

THE LAST MIRACLE of Jesus before His death was, in some respects, the most beautiful and touching of all. It was a fitting and lovely climax to that long series of gracious and healing miracles. His first miracle was wrought at the marriage in Cana of Galilee. It was done at an occasion of joy and mirth and happiness. This last miracle was done in the shadows of Gethsemane, a time and a place of sorrow and travail of soul and agony. Against this dark background shines the beauty of Christ's last miracle.

When Jesus worked His first miracle at Cana of Galilee and turned water into wine, the astonished governor of the feast, when he had tasted the wine, called the bridegroom and said to him, "Every man at the beginning doth set forth good wine; . . . then that which is worse: but thou hast kept the good wine until now." So it might be said concerning the miracles of Jesus. He kept the best wine, the best miracle, until the last. It was a miracle done when He was suffering. It was done not in response to a cry for pity and help from some troubled soul, but in answer to the blow of an enemy. Jesus said, "Love your enemies, bless them that curse you, do good to them that hate you, and pray for them which despitefully use you, and persecute you." This was His great text, and here in Gethsemane is His great illustration of the text. He practiced what He preached.

All four Gospels relate the fact that when Jesus was seized by His enemies in the Garden of Gethsemane, one of His disciples drew a sword and smote off the ear of the servant of the high priest. Only John gives us the name of that servant, Malchus, and only John gives us the name of the disciple who drew the sword, Peter. But even if the name had not been given, it would have been an easy guess that it was Peter who smote with the sword. Perhaps the authors of the other three Gospels, written earlier than John's, when many of the actors in the scenes of that last night were still alive, felt it would be a protection to Peter not to give his name, whereas John, writing much later, felt it would be safe then to give the name of Peter. Only Luke among the four Gospels gives us the account of this last miracle, how Jesus put forth His hand and touched the man's ear and healed him.

The supper was over. The traitor had gone out into the night with Satan in his heart to betray Jesus. The farewell address had been spoken. The sublime intercessory prayer had been offered, and a closing hymn had been sung. Then Jesus led the eleven disciples down the road and across the bridge over the brook Kedron, and up the other side into the Garden of Gethsemane, where He left eight of the disciples near the gate and, with Peter and James and John, went farther into the Garden. There, charging them to watch with Him, He removed Himself from them a stone's cast, and entered into His agony. Now He was coming out of that agony. Coming to the disciples for the third time, and finding them asleep again, He said, "Sleep on now, and take your rest." Then, in a moment He spoke another word, "Rise, let us be going: behold, he is at hand that doth betray me."

Presently the mob, led by Judas, their torches dancing in the night, pressed through the gate of the Garden seeking their prey. Facing the mob, Jesus said to them, "Whom seek ye?" They answered, "Jesus of Nazareth." Jesus said to them, "I am he." When they heard that, the mob recoiled and fell to the ground. For a moment the majesty of the Son of God overcame them. Then, recovering themselves, they gathered about Jesus to seize Him. At that, Peter drew his sword, and aiming it at one whom he had seen strike Jesus, and who was the servant of the high priest, he smote off his ear. At once Jesus said to Peter: "Put up again thy sword into his place: for all they that take the sword shall perish with the sword. Thinkest thou that I cannot now pray to my Father, and he shall

presently give me more than twelve legions of angels? . . .
The cup which my father hath given me, shall I not drink
it?" Then He stretched forth His hand and touched the
ear of Malchus and healed him. So with this beautiful act
of mercy and forgiveness the book of the miracles of Jesus
comes to a close.

Violence and the Gospel of Christ

Peter was loyal to his Master that night when he drew
that sword, and you can hardly keep from cheering him
when you see him strike that blow in defense of his Master. He was loyal, but he was mistaken. That night, before they had gone out into the Garden, Jesus had said,
"He that hath no sword, let him sell his garment, and buy
one." Peter understood Jesus in a literal sense; but evidently Jesus was speaking figuratively, meaning that the
lives of all the disciples would be filled with difficulty and
hardship, and everywhere they would confront the opposition of the world. The Koran promises sensual joys and
pleasures in heaven for all Moslems who die in battle in
defense of their faith. The Moslem conquests were spread
over the world with fire and sword. The Christians, in a
certain sense, repaid the Moslems in kind in the Crusades, those strange and, in some respects, glorious phe-
nomena of the Middle Ages.

Yet the Crusades in their use of the sword were a
complete departure from the Spirit of Christ. It is not
without significance that what those mailed knights of
the Crusades were fighting for was an empty tomb. The
real Christ can never be found with the sword. On one
occasion when Jesus had received some discourtesy from
a Samaritan village, his two disciples, the two Sons of
Thunder, James and John, came to Him and said, "Lord,
wilt thou that we command fire to come down from heaven,
and consume them, even as Elias did?" But Jesus turned
and rebuked them and said, "Ye know not what manner
of spirit ye are of. For the Son of man is not come to
destroy men's lives, but to save them."

There are few hymns that we like to sing better than
Toplady's "Rock of Ages" and Charles Wesley's "Jesus,

Lover of My Soul." Toplady was a strong Calvinist, and got into a dispute with John Wesley over that great doctrine of God's sovereignty and election. Wesley caricatured Toplady's doctrine in these words, "One and twenty of mankind are elected. Nineteen in twenty are reprobated. The elect shall be saved, do what they will; the reprobate shall be damned, do what they can. Reader, believe this or be damned. Witness my hand, Augustus Toplady." To this unworthy caricature Toplady responded with a pamphlet in which he called Wesley "a perverter of the Truth," and said that under different circumstances a similar forgery would have landed him in Virginia or Maryland.

Of the same sad nature was a dispute between Newman Smith and the great Baptist preacher Robert Hall. In a controversy with Hall on some religious point, Smith wrote a bitter pamphlet, denouncing Hall and his doctrine. Unable to select what he thought was just the appropriate title, he sent the pamphlet to a friend upon whose judgment he relied, and asked him to suggest a suitable title. Some time before, Newman Smith had written a widely read and very helpful pamphlet, "Come to Jesus." When his friend read this bitter tirade against Hall, he sent the pamphlet back to Smith and wrote to him, "The title which I suggest for your pamphlet is this, 'Go to Hell' by the Author of 'Come to Jesus.'" So true followers of Christ and true friends of Christ, like James and John, forget sometimes the Spirit of Christ.

Christ's Presence with His Church

This last miracle of Jesus shows His concern for and His presence with the church. An earless man would have been a sad and dreadful spectacle at the cross. But Christ prevented that spectacle by touching his ear and healing him. So He is ever with His church. Sometimes we wonder how the church has survived through the ages—how it has survived its own blunders and follies, as well as the bitter opposition and persecution of the world. The secret is that Christ has kept His promise, "Lo, I am with you always." He is ever in our midst, making reparation for the wounds, the wrong impressions, the misrepresentations, which we, His followers, make to the world. Not a sin is committed by a Christian, not a bitter word spoken, not a false or cruel act done, but the hand of Christ is there to make reparation, and heal our mistakes and misrepresentations of His Spirit

Submission to the Will of God

This final miracle of Jesus not only showed mercy and forgiveness to a foe, not only protected Peter and the others of the Twelve from the violence of the mob, not only saved Christ from misrepresentation, but also showed on the part of Jesus a beautiful and complete obedience to the will of God. Just a little before, in His sore agony, when He had sweat as it were great drops of blood, He had prayed, "If it be possible, let this cup pass from me: nevertheless not as I will, but as thou wilt." Now He knew that the cup could not pass. Only by drinking that cup could He make an atonement for the sinner. Therefore, when Peter drew the sword and smote the servant of the high priest, Jesus told him to put his sword into the sheath, saying, "The cup which my Father hath given me, shall I not drink it?"

The sword or the cup? Christ was confronted with this choice. For our eternal good, and our example, too, Jesus chose the cup and not the sword. Still His disciples are confronted at times with this same choice—the sword or the cup? Which shall we take? Shall we take the sword, and claim our right, and defend ourselves, and assail those who do us wrong? Or, following in the footsteps of Jesus, shall we refuse the sword and drink the cup?

Christian Forgiveness

This last miracle of Jesus was a sublime example of Christian forgiveness of those who do us wrong. Frequently Christ had preached that doctrine, "Love your enemies. . . . Do good to them that hate you, and pray for them which . . . persecute you." Now, at the end of His ministry, He gave a sublime example of how men ought to love their enemies. In some respects it is more wonderful and moving than the prayer He offered on the cross, "Father, forgive them; for they know not what they do." Some of those around the cross hardly understood what they were doing. But this deed of mercy and forgiveness was done to a cowardly foe, the worst kind of foe, the one who strikes a defenseless man. Even Paul, under similar circumstances, when he was on trial before the Sanhedrin, and at the command of the high priest was smitten on the face, could not come up to the measure of Jesus, but answered in indignation, "God shall smite thee, thou whited wall!"

Peter must long have remembered what Jesus said and did there that night in the Garden of Gethsemane; for long afterward he wrote to Christian disciples who were suffering at the hands of their enemies:

> If, when ye do well, and suffer for it, ye take it patiently, this is acceptable with God. For even hereunto were ye called: because Christ also suffered for us, leaving us an example, that ye should follow his steps: who did no sin, neither was guile found in his mouth: who, when he was reviled, reviled not again; when he suffered, he threatened not; but committed himself to him that judgeth righteously.

The heaviest burden that one can bear is the burden of an unforgiving spirit. It is a burden, too, which you cannot ask God to help you bear, because it is so contrary to the Spirit of Jesus. There is no greater barrier to the work of the Holy Spirit and the joy of salvation in a man's soul than to harbor the spirit of enmity, ill will, or malice toward any fellow being. Nothing takes you further from Christ than such a spirit. Nothing brings you nearer to Christ than to forgive, even as Christ forgave that man who smote him that night in the Garden of Gethsemane.

During one of the persecutions of the Armenians by the Turks, an Armenian girl and her brother were closely pursued by a bloodthirsty Turkish soldier. He trapped them at the end of a lane and killed the brother before the sister's eyes. The sister managed to escape by leaping over the wall and fleeing into the country. Later she became a nurse. One day a wounded Turkish soldier was brought into her hospital. She recognized him at once as the soldier who had killed her brother and had tried to kill her. His condition was such that the least neglect on the part of the nurse would have cost him his life. But she gave him the most painstaking and constant care. One day, when he was on the road to recovery, he recognized her as the girl whose brother he had slain. He said to her, "Why have you done this for me, who killed your brother?"

She answered, "Because I have a religion which teaches me to forgive my enemies."

I wonder if Malchus, with his healed ear, was in the crowd which stood about the cross the next day when Jesus was dying? Perhaps he was; and perhaps someone standing near him saw with surprise his emotion and said to him, "What do those three fellows, those three malefactors on the crosses, mean to you, anyway?"

Malchus may have answered, "I saw that man last night in the Garden of Gethsemane. I was with the mob that seized Him; and after Judas had kissed Him, I struck Him in the face with my fist. Then one of His disciples drew his sword and struck at me. He missed my head, but cut off my ear. And then that Man, that one there in the middle, the one crowned with thorns and covered with blood, touched my ear and healed me!"

The Raising of the Widow of Nain's Son

Martin Luther (1483–1546) was Germany's best-known preacher and religious leader. He was trained as an Augustinian monk and lectured on the Bible at the University of Wittenberg. Never satisfied with his spiritual experience, Luther found peace through the study of Paul's epistles when he discovered salvation by grace alone through faith in Jesus Christ. His opposition to the scandals relating to the sale of indulgences eventually led to the Reformation and the founding of the Lutheran Church. He was a conscientious preacher who sought to make the Bible meaningful to the common people. He wrote more than 400 works—from pamphlets to books as well as 125 hymns.

This sermon is reprinted from *The Precious and Sacred Writings of Martin Luther*, Vol. 14, edited by John Nicholas Lenker and published in 1904 by Lutherans in All Lands Co.

Martin Luther

7

THE RAISING OF THE WIDOW OF NAIN'S SON

Now when he came nigh to the gate of the city, behold, there was a dead man carried out, the only son of his mother, and she was a widow: and much people of the city was with her (Luke 7:12).

The Miracle Itself

IN THIS GOSPEL you see how the Evangelist again presents to us a divine miracle, by which he desires to move us to lift our hearts to God, in which is the same state of things as at the time existed in this woman; for today's lesson was not written for the sake of this widow, but for the instruction and help of all who should hear this gospel until the end of the world, among whom we also have been reckoned.

In the first place notice what loving-kindness and grace were shown to this woman by Christ. We must truly confess she did not merit them, for she is going out of the city with her friends, where there is nothing but crying and weeping. The good woman thought of nothing as little as that she should again lead back her son into the city alive, and for this reason she does not desire it, nor does she ask it, much less has she deserved it. She never thought of such a thing that Christ should come hither; yes, she did not at the time know Christ nor did she know anything of His helping the people. Here all merit and preparations for meeting Him are out of the question.

Now all this has been written to the end that just as here this deed of mercy befell this widow freely and entirely of grace, only because it solicited Christ's sympathy, so from this we can draw the general rule that applies to all the merciful deeds of God, that they all overtake us without our merits, even before we seek them. He lays the foundation and makes the beginning. But why does He pity us? In this way it continues to be the grace of God. Otherwise, if we deserved it, it would not be grace. And if it be of grace, then we can say to Him: You are a gracious God, You do good also to them who deserve it not.

This sermon seems easy to us, but where are they who mean it with their hearts? If we believed that everything comes to us from God's grace and mercy, we would daily run and rejoice, our hearts would continually rise and dwell in heaven. When we once get to heaven we will see that this is true. Now no one believes it. The god of this world, the Devil, has such great power on earth that we do not see the work of God nor know it (2 Cor. 4:4). Therefore we do not appreciate it, we misuse God's mercies, and are entirely unthankful to Him.

If I only kept in mind that He gave me eyes, truly a very great treasure, it would be no wonder if shame caused my death, because of my ingratitude in that I never yet thanked Him for the blessing of sight. But we do not see His noble treasures and gifts; they are too common. But when a blind babe happens to be born, then we see what a painful thing the lack of sight is, and what a precious thing even one eye is, and what a divine blessing a healthy, bright countenance is; it serves us during our whole lives, and without it one would rather be dead; and yet no one thanks God for it. Examine the entire body, and you will everywhere see traces of God's grace and goodness.

Hence Psalm 33:5 says: "The earth is full of the goodness of the Lord." He had pure eyes and could see far, that the whole world was full of the goodness and loving-kindness of God. From whom, however, has this goodness come? Have we deserved it? No, but it pleased God to cast His gifts thus promiscuously into the world, which the unthankful receive almost as freely as the thankful. We are grieved when we are obliged to throw away one or two dollars, or less, or even to give them to the poor; how much does God daily cast away of His goods into the world and no one thanks Him for anything? Yes, who even acknowledges their receipt?

Thus we may observe all creatures and become convinced of God's goodness in them. Christ says in Matthew 5:45: "He maketh his sun to rise on the evil and on the good, and sendeth rain on the just and on the unjust." As though He would say: I give it to the whole crowd; but who thanks Me a single time for it? He enlightens my and your eyes, but no one acknowledges that it is God's blessing. If some morning the sun should not rise, or rise three hours late, what distress and loss would that cause? How we would open our mouths and eyes? Then everyone would say: God be praised and thanked, who has given us such a light! But since it occurs daily, that the sun rises and shines at the appointed time, no one considers it a blessing.

So it is with the rain from heaven, with the grain in the field and with all God's creatures. They exist in such abundance, and we are daily so overwhelmed by their abundance that we fail to see them.

At times God permits some man to fall into anxiety and need, into pain and distress, so that the world seems as though it had no God, and it makes a person blind, lame, dropsical, and lets anyone die, as here the widow's son; for they are His creatures, He can do with them what He will. Now, why does He do this? He does it in such an abundance only that we may continually experience His loving-kindness.

Therefore as the disciples in John 9:2 asked the Lord concerning the man blind from his birth, whether he or his parents sinned, the Lord answered and said: "Neither hath this man sinned, nor his parents; but that the works of God should be made manifest in him." As though He would say: God desires to be praised in this blind person, for He sees that the treasures of the whole world do not move us, wherefore He floods us with His goodness out of pure grace, that He may present a blind person before our eyes for us to see what a costly treasure we have in the blessing of our sight; although we cannot recognize His grace and kindness in our fortune, that we at least might know and identify them then in our misfortune. Therefore this man had to be blind in order that the others might know themselves, and say: Alas Thou good God, what a precious gift I have, what a good thing a healthy body is and a bright countenance! But no one takes it to heart! Yes, it is true we say: have not the cows eyes also! Now, if you were blind you would of course feel the loss, which you do not now feel, because you are well and overshowered with God's blessings.

So it was in the case of this widow, in whom God lets Himself be known, as to what kind of a God He is, what He thinks of us, and what we must think of Him. This woman has two misfortunes around her neck. First, she is a widow. This is misfortune enough for one woman, that she is forsaken and alone, and has no one to whom she dare look for comfort. And therefore God in the Scriptures is often mentioned as the Father of the widow and orphans, as in Psalms 68:6 and 146:9: "God setteth the solitary in families. The Lord preserveth the strangers and orphans, he delivers the widow." Again: she has an only son about to die, who should have been her comfort. Now, God comes and takes away her husband and son. She had much better have lost house and home, yes, her own life, than her son and husband. But the Lord turns it around. While the husband lived the woman did not appreciate what a blessing a husband was; but when he died she first became aware of it. When he lived, she thought: O, other women have husbands, too! And thought her husband was like other husbands. But afterward when he was dead, she became aware what kind of a man she had lost.

So, too, when her son was bright and well, she did not appreciate the blessing of God, but as soon as he died, she then first saw what a treasure she had lost. Before she did not desire to spend on him; but now, since he is dead, she spends all she has and even herself upon him. And thus it is also with us. There are many of you who do not expend ten dollars that your child may be reared better; if the child dies the parents wish and say: O would to God he were alive, I would give many hundred dollars! Why did you not give something before that he might have learned a little? What is the reason you do not appreciate the grace and blessings of God? In short, the world remains world, and it will not change into anything else.

Now, the woman went ahead and did not know what God had given her; but she was soon obliged to experience it. For before she turns around, and she thinks she is the safest, God comes, tries the wife a little and teaches her certain things, takes her husband and her son. This all has been written for us that we might have an example and learn to acknowledge God when He blesses us with a healthy body, a bright countenance, and bestows upon us other blessings. He does not give them to the end that you should rejoice in them, but that you may know what to think of Him. When He takes a member out of your family, permits your wife to die, or destroys one of your eyes, all this is done that you may see what you have enjoyed from Him.

And this is now the common teaching through all the Gospels, that we may see what kind of a God we have. It is also shown us here in this gospel that God will forsake no one; therefore He permits the wife to see in a new light what kind of a God she has. For when she was forsaken and had neither son nor husband, then Christ manifests Himself to her and says: Learn to believe, trust God, know Him to whom death and life are alike: have a good heart, be of good courage, weep not, there is no need of it. He then goes and awakens the dead, and gives him again to his mother.

This and like miracles God does that the heart may learn how it should be disposed to Him and what it may expect from Him. As now this wife was fully convinced that there was no hope for her son, that it was impossible for her to receive him back alive again; yes, if one had said to her: Before an hour your son will be alive again, she would have regarded it as impossible and said: It is more possible for the heavens to fall than for my son to live again. Behold, here comes God before she looks around, and does what she never dared to ask of Him, as it is impossible, and He restores her son alive to her again.

But why does God do this? He permits man to fall so deeply into danger and anxiety, until no help or advice is within reach, and still He desires that we should not doubt, but trust in Him who out of an impossible thing can make something possible, and make something out of nothing. If you are so deep in sin that your heart denies you all grace and the mercy of God and makes you think there is no hope for you, as many consciences are ensnared by such anxiety and distress, then turn about and look here how friendly and graciously God allows Himself to be pictured by Christ in this gospel, that you may observe that He means it well with you from His heart; that He is not here either to condemn or excommunicate you, but to preserve your soul forever. For this purpose such miracles and wonderful works are held before our eyes, and they also serve to the end that we may see. As God here helps this widow in a temporal way through Christ, so He will help us not only bodily, but much more spiritually, and our souls forever, if we only put our hope in Him.

But all miracles and works of God are considered impossible in our eyes, and they are also impossible for the natural man to grasp; and this is to the end that God may be confessed to be an almighty Creator, who from something impossible can create something possible, and can make something out of nothing. It is impossible after I am dead that I should live again, and even if I should pray to all the angels and all the saints for it nothing will result from such prayers; what then can the free will accomplish? Nevertheless in death I should say: I shall live, not through myself, but because I know that my God is so skillful that He can make something, not out of wood that lies before my eyes, but it is His nature and way to make a thing possible here from something impossible, and create something out of nothing; otherwise He were not the true and real God.

Therefore, if death be present and I can no longer live, I must still know enough to say: Yet I live, and will live; so that death, that is all about me, is like a spark of fire, and life is as great as the sea. Now reason cannot grasp how this takes place. But whoever believes knows for a certainty that to him death will be like a spark of fire in the midst of the ocean, that is extinguished in a moment. God is almighty, he who believes is in God, therefore he is in life, and though he were in the midst of death. So too a poor person who believes thinks like this one here in death: O! poverty is a spark of fire, and wealth is as abundant as water in the sea; now a moment only is needed for poverty to sink, and I will be rich; for by faith God has entirely changed him who now has all things in his power. So also with shame; when one's good name and reputation go down, people think they will never again be regained; if you believe and hold to God, it is a matter only of a moment, and you are again in great honor. For our God knows the art that from invincible poverty He can create great riches, from great shame unexpressable honor. So it is also with sin, if you believe. Thus sin compared with righteousness is as a spark of fire compared with the whole sea of water.

This you see beautifully illustrated in the case of this woman. She is overwhelmed by exceedingly great pain and anguish, so that she thinks God, heaven, earth, and all things are opposed to her. And since she looks into this with the eyes of sense, sees it as it is before her natural eyes, she must conclude it is impossible for her to be delivered from her great anxiety. But when her son was raised from the dead for her, she was as though the whole heaven and earth, wood and stone, and everything laughed and rejoiced with her; then she forgot all pain and suffering, this wholly disappeared just like a spark of fire is extinguished when it falls into the sea. Therefore it is written in the prophet Isaiah 64:6–8: "For Jehovah hath called thee as a wife forsaken and grieved in spirit, even a wife of youth when she is cast off, saith thy God. For a small moment have I forsaken thee; but with great mercies will I gather thee. In overflowing wrath I hid my face from thee for a moment; but with everlasting lovingkindness will I have mercy on thee, saith Jehovah thy Redeemer."

But this I do not see, I think this moment is an eternal something before God; but it is in truth only a moment; and much joy follows as Psalm 8:5 also says: "For thou hast made him but little lower than God, and crownest him with glory and honor." But this is still all hid from us, and we do not see it as this wife does. Her departed son is in the midst of life, for God has him in His bosom, and intends to wake him. There is a spark of death there that surrounds him, which no one saw. But now when he became alive that was revealed which before was hidden from the whole world.

Thus God certainly deals also with us. Here we should learn the kind of God we have, namely, He who surrounds us and is about us in our very greatest dangers and troubles. Therefore, if one is poor, sticks deep in sin, lies in death, is in sorrows and other afflictions, he thinks: it is a transition state, it is a drop and a spark; for God has surrounded him on all sides with pure wealth, righteousness, life and joy, only He does not permit him to see it. But it is a matter of only a little time when we shall see and enjoy it. Thus you have here an example, not of faith, but of the pure grace and loving-kindness of God. Now we must also say a little on the spiritual understanding or the allegorical interpretation of today's gospel.

The Spiritual Interpretation of This Miracle

All works and miracles that Christ does visibly and publicly should be interpreted to the end that they may show forth the works which He does among men unseen and spiritually or within them. Therefore this bodily death signifies the spiritual death of the soul, which man must believe. For no one can see into the soul of another while we live; but when we are dead, we then have other eyes, then we see that the whole world is dead. Therefore the Lord spoke to a Pharisee, Matthew 8:22, who first wanted to go and bury his father: "Follow me, and leave the dead to bury their own dead."

This youth who is here being borne to his grave is bodily dead. But there are also some inwardly dead before God who still live here in the body. The soul is dead that does not believe in God and cleave to Him. And even though he be in the midst of death, yet he lives, as I said above.

This spiritual death occurs in a twofold manner: some are dead in their souls, but no one sees that death as we see bodily death, and this woman herself neither sees nor feels it. So the whole world is dead, but it realizes it not. Therefore some are also spiritually dead, who feel it well enough, as those whom the law has terribly punished. We do not here speak of those who care nothing for spiritual death; but of those who feel that they are dead and that their hearts tremble, and who feel in their consciences that they have unbelieving hearts. He is dead quite otherwise than he who does not feel it, and yet always lives in wantonness. Now the one who does not experience his unbelief cannot be helped, for he does not know his sickness, and lives on, cares nothing for God nor the world. But he who feels this death suffers misery and distress, there is struggling and despair, the world becomes too confined for him, he seeks assistance and advice, he despises neither stone nor wood when they can afford him counsel, not to say that he should hear anything of man, even of the most insignificant person.

Who now gives him this feeling. The law does it, in that it reveals sin. The law says: "Thou shalt have no other gods." When I hear this, I must and should do it, but I cannot. Then I quickly conclude that I am condemned. When I act thus, death comes immediately and there is such a struggle in my heart that if I should receive no help I would have to remain forever in this death and struggle. This then is the death of the only son, who lies in the bier, the pallbearers are continually carrying him into hell.

The pallbearers are the preachers of the law, who do nothing else than plunge mankind ever deeper and deeper into death; as those here hasten to the grave with the dead they are the more terrified and driven the deeper into perdition. It never becomes better with mankind, yes, it is ever growing worse.

This we have thoroughly experienced under the pope, in our confession of and in our making satisfaction for sin. We allowed ourselves to think we would atone for our sins by good works, but it was only an anxiety of the conscience. Thus we ever sank deeper toward hell. Hence, when you have people who fear sin and condemnation, they are already dead; you dare not preach to these much more of the law, you must show them the way of salvation and preach to them the Gospel. When our papists meet such troubled souls, they refer them to rosaries, to pilgrimages, to this and that work; but one helps like the other.

The pallbearers would have still moved on and laid the deceased in his grave and buried him, had Christ not come, so Christ must come also here with His Word and grace. And this now is that other office of the Gospel, which does not teach what you are to do, but whence you are to receive help, that you may do it, as Christ does here. He asks not, what is here? or how do you do this? do you wish to have the youth restored to life again, and the like? He asks none of these things, but He has mercy on the mother, goes to her, touches the bier, and the bearers soon stand still. That is, when man preaches the goodness of God, and when Christ presents us with His merits and works, then the hand is laid upon the coffin, and the bearers stand still; that is, you no longer hear the preachers of the law, you no longer believe them, but you say: preach works here, preach works there, we have a different sermon. While our hands are on the coffin they accomplished nothing; the dead does not come to life again; but when Christ's hand touches the coffin the mighty work is done. For when men hear that Christ's work does it, and that His works are presented to us, they say: What need we to do beside? For here our doing is useless and in vain.

But the dead will not be raised to life so quickly. The Word of God is of course preached to us, the goodness of God and whatever is given us through Christ; but this is not yet sufficient, this is only first touching the coffin. The voice of Christ in the heart must also be added, that we may believe the Word, that it is really as we preach. The youth does not immediately arise after he is touched, but when the Lord spoke: "Young man, I say unto thee, Arise!" This voice stirred the heart and caused the dead to rise to life. When I in like manner hear the Word, and allow human traditions to move me, men still bear me ever on and I ever remain in distress; it helps me little. I must besides the external sermon also hear this voice in the heart: "Young man, I say unto thee, Arise:" that is, I must believe this sermon, cleave to it with my heart, trust in it, and let neither sin, death, devil, nor hell draw me from it.

Thus we have two sermons. One lays the hand on the bier. This does not yet accomplish anything. But the other, when the hand is laid on the coffin and the voice follows in the heart, this accomplishes all. The first proclaims to us the works of Christ, how they are done for us and given to us. But when the voice is heard in the heart, then the one who was before dead begins to speak and to confess the faith with his mouth which he believes and feels in his heart. That is, when the heart believes, the work of love follows, namely, that you speak, that is, preach to others and thank God for the blessing and faith He has shown and given to you.

From this follows great joy and thanksgiving, by which God is praised and exalted, just as here a great report about Christ went over the entire land of the Jews and into all the neighboring countries. Thus a Christian can lead many to faith. Therefore man should not make a work of jugglery out of miracles and wonders, as the papists have done.

This is said on today's gospel, in which we see how God helps and saves us, moved by pure grace and loving-kindness, without any merit or worthiness whatever on our part, yes, before we seek or request help from Him. God grant that we may believe this!

The Woman of Canaan

John Ker (1819–1886) is little known today, but in his day he was a respected preacher and professor of preaching and pastoral work at the United Free Church Seminary in Glasgow, Scotland. He published two volumes of sermons.

This one is from the *Sermons Second Series*, published in Edinburgh in 1888 by David and Douglas.

John Ker

8

THE WOMAN OF CANAAN

Then Jesus answered and said unto her, O woman, great is thy faith: be it unto thee even as thou wilt (Matthew 15:28).

WHEN OUR LORD JESUS CHRIST lived on earth, He did not carry His mission beyond the Land of Promise. He has given the reason of this: "I, if I be lifted up from the earth, will draw all men unto me." He must first ascend His cross, and then ascend His throne, that divine love and power, His gospel and His spirit, might be ready to move forth with the command that "repentance and remission of sins should be preached among all nations, beginning at Jerusalem." But in His journeyings He came, ever and again, into gracious contact with mankind—sinners from beyond the Jewish pale, that He might show Gentile and Samaritan what was in His heart. He traveled close on the borderline of heathendom, that the light of His presence might shine across on some of the longing souls that were in darkness and the shadow of death. In one of these walks of compassion He came near the coasts of Tyre and Sidon, where the remnants of those nations dwelt which had been driven from their land for their sins.

One of this race, a woman of Canaan, was suffering from a sore affliction in her family, and she sought Him out and followed Him with an urgent prayer for help. At first He turned a deaf ear to her and repelled her petition with a coldness which rises into what seems harshness. But He knew the strength of faith which was in her heart, and He wished to bring it out for the perfecting of her own spiritual nature, and for an example to us. When at last her faith appeared in its marvelous strength and beauty, He looked on it with wonder. It is said of the first creation, "God saw it, and behold, it was very good"; and of the second, "The Lord Jehovah shall be satisfied in his works." And so, when a part of this new creation appears in a human heart, Christ sees of the travail of His soul and is satisfied. It is an earnest of the joy set before Him, for which He endured the Cross and despised the shame. We shall make the faith of this woman the subject of thought by trying to answer two questions: First, what made her faith so remarkable? Second, what enabled her to hold on and at last to triumph? We shall thus have a view of it first on its outward, and then on its inward side.

What Made the Faith
of This Woman So Remarkable?

The first thing which strikes us is that she had much against her in *her original circumstances*. She was, as you see, a woman of Canaan. She was not of the Jewish race, nor even, as it would seem, a proselyte; but an "alien from the commonwealth of Israel and a stranger to the covenants of promise." She was not only a Gentile, but of that family of Gentiles which must have had most dislike to the Jews. Her forefathers had suffered from their hostility, and she no doubt had felt their haughty bigotry and exclusiveness. There was a frontier line of dislike to cross, far wider than any distance between Tyre and Palestine. But it did not keep her from finding her way to the great Teacher of the Jewish nation.

Then, think of how her circumstances must have affected her knowledge. She addresses Christ as Lord, with reverence and trust, and speaks of Him as the Son of David. But how dim was her light, compared with that of those who had heard the Scriptures read in their synagogues, who had joined in the services and sacrifices of the temple, and had been prepared for the coming of Christ as a Savior from sin and sorrow! How little did she know compared with Anna, the prophetess who departed not from the temple night and day, with Martha and Mary, who heard His words in their own home, or even with that woman in the city who was a sinner, who had listened to Him without, and was then drawn into Simon's house to weep until her heart was like to break! All these had remarkable faith, but we do not know of any who had so little knowledge on which to base it, and so little room to take home the promise to their own case. It is an instance of faith like a grain of mustard seed which can remove mountains, or wing its way over them.

God has bestowed on man two great powers: reason and faith. They are not opposed to each other, though they are sometimes spoken of as if they were. But they are very different. The field of reason is the things which are seen and temporal; the field of faith, the things which are unseen and eternal. Where reason can go no farther, faith passes forward on stronger than angels' wings, grasping the hand of God; where reason is blind, faith has eyes for a world in which it dwells, like those men of old who lived as seeing Him who is invisible. Let us thank God for reason, but let us thank Him above all for faith, for the power by which the soul can find a way through all the thick folds of matter straight to the living God, and, through small privileges and what to us seems hard treatment, can find out Christ and fall at His feet with the burden of its need.

It is often impossible for us to ascertain the laws by which faith operates, and the ground on which, in individual cases, its strength rests. Its object is unseen, and so also is its work in the soul; but its effects are very sure and palpable. "The wind bloweth where it listeth, and we hear the sound thereof, but cannot tell whence it cometh, and whither it goeth"; but we can judge of its power in the barriers it breaks down, and of its sweetness when it comes to wake up flowers and blossoms.

Some of us may have seen it in poor, lone, agonized sufferers who held fast to their hope in God and repelled every doubt, and we wondered how their faith had learned to begin and maintain its hold. It was the "good pleasure of his goodness, and the work of faith with power." The case of this woman is one of these. What are many of our arguments but doubts answering doubts, the taking and retaking of outposts, when she and others like her pass right into the citadel through all obstacles and enemies, and claim for themselves Him who alone can help a stricken spirit! "They shall come from the east, and from the west, and from the north, and from the south, and shall sit down in the kingdom of God." "And, behold, there are last which shall be first, and there are first which shall be last."

Another thing which made the faith of this woman remarkable was that she had little countenance from Christ's disciples. It is very strange to see the burning love of the disciples to the souls of men after the ascension of Christ compared with their coldness while He Himself was with them. Think of how they pleaded with men to come to Him as a Prince and a Savior, while in His lifetime they often surrounded Him like an icy wall! It becomes clear to those who consider it that something very decisive had happened in the interval to change their views of Christ's relation to men. Nothing less than His death and resurrection and the disclosure of His purposes of mercy can account for this.

Observe them here—they do not, indeed, rebuke the woman as they rebuked the parents who brought their children to Christ; they only ask Him to send her away. In all charity let us hope that they wished her request to be granted; but the reason they give takes the heart out of their petition—"for she crieth after us." It appears to be not so much sympathy with her sorrow as annoyance at her importunity, and a desire to be freed from the trouble of her presence. No doubt she felt it, felt that they looked on her as an annoyance and a shame to them, and that they would gladly be quit of her, in the way some cast an alms to a persistent beggar. Weaker faith would have felt the chill which surrounded Him, and would have retired. But it is not from them that she expects an answer. She will take it from none but Christ Himself and she presses past the disciples into His presence—"Lord, to whom but to Thee?"

And is there not a lesson here for us Christians as to the spirit in which we should deal with those who are, as it is called, outside? Are we approaching them in the spirit of the disciples before the day of Pentecost, or after it; with the heart of those to whom the Cross of Christ had as yet no meaning, or of those to whom it opened the infinite sympathy and long-suffering of God? If we carry the Gospel to men with no pity in our own souls for their misery, but merely to quiet the disturbance of their cries, to preserve social order, and to save ourselves and society from danger, we cannot expect great progress in our works. Men know very well when a gift comes from a loving heart, and when it is thrown to them to get ease for ourselves.

God did not cast down His benefits from the door of heaven; He came down to earth with His heart in them, and this makes the difference between a benefit and a blessing. If we are to win men we must go to them in Christ's spirit and, as it were, in His person. "As though God did beseech you by us; we pray you in Christ's stead, be ye reconciled to God."

And yet if there are any who keep back from Christ, because, as they say, Christians are so cold and inconsistent, let them know from the example of this woman that they are not thereby excused. Christ invites them to come to Himself to judge of Him not by what His disciples do, but by what He Him has said and done. "Look unto me"— "Come unto me, all ye that labor and are heavy laden"— "Him that cometh to me I will in no wise cast out." It is to Him at last we have to give in our account, and we cannot be justified in our rejection of Him, until we have taken our decisive answer from no lips but His own.

And yet here the woman's faith reaches its greatest trial, in *the conduct of Christ*. The disciples, cold as they are, seem merciful compared with their Master. She breaks through outward difficulties to find an iron wall about His heart. The story is so told that we can see it in each appeal, and each repulse. As she cries, and pours her heart into her prayer, He is moving away from her with silent neglect. "He answered her not a word," as if she were not only beneath help but beneath being soothed or spoken to.

Have we not sometimes felt this ourselves, when we have prayed to God in our trouble? He not only withheld the deliverance we asked, but left us all alone with our bitter, helpless cries. That dreadful silence of God! It is harder to many a poor heart than the sorest word which can be spoken: "O Lord my rock; be not silent to me: lest, if thou be silent to me, I become like them that go down into the pit." If He would only speak, though it were to reprove me, I could bear it. "Show me wherefore thou contendest with me." Anything but this stony silence, this desolate forsakenness which gathers around me, and makes me ask if there be a God who cares for me at all.

This woman must have felt it when He answered her not a word. Still she cried after Him, and at last He spoke. But His words, were they not harder than His silence? For He did not speak to her, but only of her, and what He said appears to quench all hope. "He answered and said, I am not sent but unto the lost sheep of the house of Israel." The Son of Man is come to seek and to save the lost, but there is a chosen flock, beyond which He cannot meanwhile go.

"Then came she and worshiped Him, saying, Lord, help me." She bent before Him, cast herself on the ground to bar His way, and so she waits an answer. Does she drop the title "Son of David," as if it told against one who belonged to the Gentile race; or is it the emotion of her heart which makes her words pass into broken sobs, "Lord, help me"? At length she draws an answer from Him to herself: "It is not meet to take the children's bread, and to cast it to dogs."

Are these the words of Jesus Christ? They startle us who know the close of the contest between Him and this suppliant creature; and how must they have been listened to by those who did not know the end—with wonder by the disciples, with sinking of heart by the woman? What can she do, but rise and leave in anguish, if not in anger? "I have prayed in vain. Thy gifts be to Thyself; this boasted deliverer is as hard as He is helpless." So it would have been with ordinary human nature, so it might have been with many a one of us.

But Christ knew what was in her soul, and His own hand was upholding her against His words. "Though Abraham was ignorant of her, though Israel acknowledged her not," the faith of Abraham was in her heart,

and she had the spirit of that night-wrestler who con-
tended with the Angel of the covenant and prevailed: "I
will not let thee go until thou bless me." And she said,
"Truth, Lord: yet the dogs eat of the crumbs which fall
from their masters' table."

It is marvelous. There is a faith, a humility, a sacred
ingenuity in her reply which has no higher example in
the Word of God. A dog, yet the dog has a place in the
house, and has its claim on the master's care. She yields
all, and in the same moment gains all. It was for this
victory Christ was waiting, and He welcomed it and gave
her her heart's desire: "O woman, great is thy faith: be it
unto thee even as thou wilt." And when He grants it, He
raises her from the ground and seats her at the table and
gives her the children's bread. And now, as of another
woman, it may be said, "Wheresoever this gospel shall be
preached throughout the whole world, this also that she
hath done shall be spoken of for a memorial of her." Nor
is it written for her sake alone; but for us also it is written, "The humble shall see this and be glad; and your
heart shall live that seek God."

What Helped Her Faith to Hold On and Triumph?

We shall now, as it were, turn a page and look at the
inner side, if we may discover what helped her faith to
hold on and triumph. We do not speak of the first cause of
all, which was Christ's eye watching her steps, and His
hand bearing her up. It is impossible to exclude the divine
nature of Christ in considering the way in which He deals
with souls. It is this which saves His conduct from the
charge of hardness, and of unnecessary exposure of them
to fatal peril. He knew what was in them by His own
grace, and He knew that it could be maintained. What
the psalmist felt was, no doubt, true of her: "My soul
followeth hard after thee; thy right hand upholdeth me."
We do greatly err if we think that, when we seek God, we
are self-sustained. It is He who holds us up and guides us
to find Himself. It is not, however, of this first cause we
speak, but of the mediate causes by which this woman's
faith was upheld.

One of the first was that *she had a deep home and heart sorrow*. Her daughter lay at home grievously vexed with a devil. A malignant disease with torturing pangs had seized her child, pointing directly to the power of the Wicked One, who was permitted to make his hand more open in the face of Him who came to challenge his power.

Even yet there are calamities which speak more distinctly than others of the disorder sin has brought into our world. We sometimes see suffering so deep, so long, so apparently meaningless that we cannot connect it with any natural order of things, or with a moral government in a sinless state. We must say, "An enemy hath done this; this is the hour and the power of darkness." There is, indeed, no ground for connecting special suffering with special sin; we have been warned against this; but we may very well believe that sin is sometimes permitted to show its effects in terrible shapes, that we may be driven by the sight to the only refuge.

It was so with this woman. She had in her home and heart a terrible and constant affliction. She had tried man's skill, and it had failed. She had called on her country's gods, on Baal and Ashtaroth, but they were as deaf as in the days of old Elijah. If she had known of Epicurus with his divinities above the clouds who do not trouble themselves with human sorrow, or of the pitiless Fate of the Stoics who bid us submit to the inevitable, would it have quieted her heart when it was agonized by her daughter's moans?

But a new name was now heard in the world, a wonderful soul of compassion seemed to be moving among human diseases and sorrows, and word of it had crossed the heathen border and reached her ears. Something told her that, if what she had heard were true, there was hope here, after despair—a plank of deliverance after utter shipwreck. It was this which nerved her hand to cling. Can she go back to her dreary home and look on her daughter's convulsions and listen, helpless, to her cries? The torture of her child is in her heart, pleads through her, and presses her petition until it is granted.

And when she gains it she secures a blessing for herself. For saving faith begins oftentimes in some crisis of the life in which the soul casts itself on Christ as far as He is known, and then it learns to trust Him with all. The door of hope in the valley of Achor becomes an entrance to Him who says, "I am the door: by me if any man enter in, he shall be saved"; and so this woman returned to a changed home with a changed heart.

Now, if there be any with trouble in the soul for which they have found as yet no cure, is it not for this it has been sent? It may be some shadow of fear or grief thrown in from without; it may be some deep wound of the conscience when sin is realized in its guilt; some fainting of the spirit before the yawning hollow of a world in which there is no divine Friend; whatever it be, do not let it quit its hold of you until you have laid hold of the great Helper.

Beware of forgetting it, of having it drowned in the world's noise, or discouraged by seeming delays. If you have some grief where all other help has failed, turn your ear inward until the sense of it urges the appeal, Lord, help me! The greater the feeling of the trouble, the more surely will it carry you into the presence of the only Savior.

There are easy paths in life when men feel as if they could do without a God, and there are smooth speeches of the conscience when they persuade themselves they do not need the ransom of a Redeemer; but when the heart is convulsed with grief, when the conscience is stirred into storm, the deep currents of the soul will bear men, if they will yield to them, on to Jesus Christ, and to none but Him.

Next, this woman's faith was strong because she *had learned to take a very humble view of herself.* She has no plea but, Have mercy on me! no appeal but to her misery, with that upcast look to Christ's face, Lord help me! And when He seems to spurn her and take up the language of the common Jew who spoke of the Gentile as a dog, she accepts the name, and founds an argument upon it. The reproachful word has nothing in it which she had not felt in her own heart.

How she got her spirit of humility it is impossible to say. God's Spirit must have been her teacher, and His first lesson is to convince of sin. There are times when a soul enlightened by God feels that nothing can be said of it which it is not ready to say of itself. We have made such a miserable return to God; we have so defaced and defiled the nature He gave us; such mean and selfish and unholy thoughts have festered and swarmed within us, that the words of the psalmist rise to our lips, "'So foolish was I and ignorant; I was as a beast before thee.' These poor dumb creatures do their part in the world better than I. I am higher, and so I have made myself lower. If I could only yield to God the unquestioning obedience, the affectionate trustfulness which a dog yields to its master, how much worthier a place I should fill in the world than now I do!" Some of us may have felt this; which of us should not feel it? but who could bear to be told it, and to answer, Truth, Lord?

But, then, there is the dignity of human nature! Does not the Bible say, Remember this, and show yourselves men? And it is true; but to show ourselves men in God's sight is to humble ourselves. An old writer has said, "There are times when we must be a man, and no worm, but there are times when we must be a worm, and no man." To come into the view of that infinite purity and be abased, is the only way to rise to it.

We are on the path to the dignity of human nature when we see the indignity we have done to God and to ourselves. It is not until the prodigal sees his sin and shame among the husks and swine that he comes to himself—to his true and proper self—remembers his sonship, and says, "I will arise and go to my father." As humility goes deep down, faith rises up high and strong, for humility furnishes the roots by which faith holds on.

If you would come to Christ, you must let humility take faith by the hand and lead it to Him, and then He will lead faith to God, and open to it all the treasure-house of grace: "For thus saith the high and lofty One that inhabiteth eternity, whose name is Holy: I dwell in the high and holy place, with him also that is of a contrite and humble spirit." It is by this wonderful *also*—with him *also*—that faith passes from defeat, and even from despair, to victory. If we could but use the word *yet* as she uses it, we should, like her, gain all when we surrender all. "Truth, Lord; yet!" "I am poor and needy, yet the Lord thinketh upon me." "I said, I am cast out of thy sight; yet I will look again toward thy holy temple."

Lastly, her faith was so strong because it *had hold of another Christ, greater and more merciful than her eyes saw.* But for this, she could never have persevered—unless her soul, by some secret reasoning or divinely-given instinct, had found out a heart of sympathy beneath the looks and words which covered it. We cannot help poring over the narrative, and wondering if there was any ray of hope allowed to escape through the thick folds of indifference in which He had wrapped Himself—any board or broken piece of the ship to cling to in her death-struggle. Was it possible to draw comfort from the way in which He speaks of the Jews? With all their gainsaying and rebellion, they are still "the children."

Or is it possible that there was something in the word *dogs* being a diminutive, and having a touch of pity in it? It is the "little dogs," which belong to the house, and are therefore the objects of kindly care. Certain it is that her woman's heart seized this point, and that through the chink her faith glided into His heart's citadel, and gained the day. She could not have found it had He not left it open. Or were there not suppressed undertones of pity which her heart, rather than her ear, caught trembling in His voice—relenting looks of sympathy which her soul, more than her eye, saw in His face, breaking beforehand like sunbeams through a cloud they are about to scatter?

In any case we know that she had already learned some things about Christ which her faith could use as a support under her repulse. She had heard of His works and how He had helped others. She knew something of His errand as the Son of David. There was a reasoning of the heart which told her that a mercy like His could not be limited to place or nation, and so she set her trust in His nature above the coldness of His demeanor, and cast herself at His feet in the spirit of the ancient sufferer, "Though he slay me, yet will I trust in him."

In what way soever she had learned it, her faith went beyond appearances, and fixed on something in Christ which her soul told her must be true and real; in some such way as the needle will turn to the pole, though testing fingers may turn it aside, and winds blow and thwart it in its struggle. If you ask, as Nicodemus did, How can these things be? We can only answer, God has so made the soul of man. There is a world of atoms and forces with their gravitating law; but there is a world also of souls which has its attracting power, and which will lead those who yield to it on to the Father of spirits whose heart is felt in Jesus Christ. It leads by a way which the lion's whelps, if we may use the figure—the strong assurances of the senses—have not trodden, which the eagle's eye— the keen vision of science—has not seen; "God understandeth the way thereof, and he knoweth the place thereof"; and He can touch human souls and make them sure of the road and the end.

It is by reason of this divine gift, even in its lower form, that wherever we find men they are capable of going beyond things seen and temporal to things unseen and eternal. Those who deny these things prove, in their denial, the power to think of them. And, if we would but think deeply and tenderly, our thoughts would lead us on.

In spite of all the pressure of material laws, often so cold and crushing, there is in man what the poet calls "the heat of inward evidence, by which he doubts against the sense." The persuasion grows that there is more in the universe than he sees, and that what he does not see is better and higher, and more akin to him, than all that meets his eye. It is this which prevents men from believing, in their deepest moments, that the evil comes from God—which enables them to cling, in their sorest trials, to the faith that "Behind a frowning providence He hides a smiling face," and that, though "The Lord hath chastened me sore: but he hath not given me over unto death."

Thick thunderclouds of atheism and pessimism sometimes hang lowering over the earth, and threaten to quench all the higher hope; but God has given to the spirit a power by which it can pass up through them and sing like the lark in the sunshine and the blue sky. It is the work of the Lord Jesus Christ to educate and strengthen it by drawing it, often through much tribulation, to Himself. This history has been given to us as a glass wherein we may see the way in which He deals with many souls still, that we may not think some strange thing has happened to us in the trial of our faith, and that we may hope to the end for the grace He will bring. He gives faith ground for trusting Him, tries it whether it will trust Him with all, hides Himself that it may find Him, puts difficulties in its way that it may break through them, makes Himself stern that it may wrestle with Him, and then, when He yields, faith is stronger, and a grander Christ is revealed than the eye had seen.

His aim is to bring faith to the resolve of another daughter of the Gentiles long before: "Entreat me not to leave thee, or to return from following after thee: for whither thou goest, I will go; and where thou lodgest, I will lodge: where thou diest, will I die, and there will I be buried: the Lord do so to me, and more also, if aught but death part thee and me"; or to the clearer resolve of the apostle, who saw through death to life: "Whether I live, I live unto the Lord: or whether I die, I die unto the Lord; living or dying, I am the Lord's."

And now that we have looked at the hindrances and helps to the faith of this woman, let us put her example to its use. First, let us give our souls into the hand of Christ, as we have been taught clearly how to do, knowing Him whom we trust, and being persuaded that He is able to keep that which we commit unto Him; and then let us confide to Him every care and trial, whether they touch our outward or our inward lives. Let us go with humble thoughts of self, and high thoughts of Him; and let us hold on in trust amidst delays and seeming repulses. He conceals His purpose for a while, to surprise us with more than we could ask or think.

We read of Joseph that before he made himself known to his brethren, "he made himself strange . . . and spake roughly unto them, and . . . turned himself about from them and wept; and returned to them again, and communed with them." When we call up the scene we sometimes wonder if their hearts did not yearn to his, though it was hidden under that Egyptian mantle; and although the tears were dried on his face, and his voice made cold again, did they not whisper to themselves, "May not this be Joseph, our long-lost brother?"

Nature has wonderful instincts, but grace is still more marvelous and sure. If we have learned to know the Divine Friend even in a dim and feeble way, it will help us to wait for Him when He is under the veil of strange and stern events, until His voice is recognized from out of the cloud : "It is I, be not afraid." And then we shall receive Him gladly, and be immediately at the land where faith passes into blessed vision: "Ye now have sorrow; but I will see you again, and your heart shall rejoice, and your joy no man taketh from you." Wherefore, "Wait on the Lord; be of good courage, and He shall strengthen thine heart: wait, I say, on the Lord."

NOTES

Saving Faith

Amzi Clarence Dixon (1854–1925) was a Baptist preacher who ministered to several congregations in the south before becoming pastor of the Moody Memorial Church in Chicago (1906–1911). He left Chicago to pastor the famous Metropolitan Tabernacle in London, "Spurgeon's Tabernacle" (1911–1919). He died in 1925 while pastoring the University Baptist Church, Baltimore, Maryland. A close associate of R. A. Torrey, Dixon helped him edit *The Fundamentals*. Dixon was a popular preacher in both Britain and America.

This message is from *Through Night to Morning*, published in 1913.

Amzi Clarence Dixon

9

SAVING FAITH

Thy faith hath saved thee (Luke 18:42).

FAITH IS THE CHANNEL of blessing from God to man, just as faith is the channel of blessing from physician to patient, from government to subject, and from parent to child. If the patient has no faith in the physician, his remedies will do little good. If a citizen has no faith in the government, he is apt to resist its authority, and cut himself off from its blessings. If the child has no faith in the parent, there is little chance of the parent's molding the child's character for good. Everything that is worth saving is saved by faith. Take away faith in the government, in the family, in the bank, in the railroad corporation, in the church, and these institutions will fall to pieces of their own weight. Faith is the cement that binds their parts together.

Now God applies this universal principle to the realm of salvation. We are saved by faith. Without our faith God can be neither Physician, Father, nor King. Unbelief destroys the channel of blessing. Let us study the faith of Bartimeus and we shall see the kind of faith that saves.

It Is a Faith That Realizes Its True Condition

Bartimaeus was a beggar and blind. He had doubtless known better days. The fact that his father Timaeus is mentioned in Mark 10:46 suggests that his family may have been one of note. He might have come to Christ and commended himself on the ground of his former wealth and position in society. He might have said, "It is true that I am a beggar, but I am not one of the common beggars; there is good blood in my veins. I am proud of my ancestors." There was no masquerading in false finery. He came in the rags of a beggar; he made a beggar's plea. He was willing to confess what he was.

And until the sinner has that sort of faith in himself, he is not apt to have saving faith in Christ. While he comes excusing his sin, or apologizing for it, he need not expect salvation. When a real sinner meets the real Savior the result is real salvation. There is no use in covering the rags with a sham cloak of hypocrisy. God can see through it.

> Just as I am, without one plea,
> But that Thy blood was shed for me,
> And that Thou bid'st me come to Thee,
> O Lamb of God, I come.

> Just as I am, poor, wretched, blind,
> Sight, riches, healing of the mind,
> Yea, all I need in Thee to find,
> O Lamb of God, I come.

Matthew tells us there were two blind men. Bartimaeus only is mentioned by Mark and Luke, because he was the one whom everybody knew. He had a fellowship of suffering with his more obscure brother. It is to his credit, however, that he did not organize a blind man's club for the preservation and propagation of blindness. Such things exist today. I heard not long ago of an infidel club. That means, of course, that some men who are blind to God and His truth have organized for the purpose of cultivating blindness and shutting out the light from themselves and others. They are poor blind beggars and proud of it. It is a pitiful sight. Christ can do nothing for them until they begin to desire a better condition and come to Him for healing.

It Is a Faith That Inquires

Bartimaeus heard the stir that Christ was making among the people. There was a crowd surging along the highway after Him. Hearing the multitudes pass by he asked what it meant. The multitude then, as now, are interested in Jesus. "The common people heard Him gladly." When the real Christ appears among the people, they are not indifferent to His claims. The real Jesus sympathizes with the weak and the oppressed. When such a Savior is preached in the pulpit, the people come to hear Him.

He has made a stir in the world. If we will listen we can hear in history the tramp of the multitude that follow Him. In the literary world His name inspires the best poetry and prose. In the world of commerce He is felt. When Carey went to India, there was not a grammar of the language. When Morrison went to China, he found no helps for the study of their difficult tongue. Missionaries of the Cross were the only ones who would take the time, and give their strength to mastering difficult languages in order that they might convey to the people the message of salvation through Christ. As a result, the nations of the world are now joined in commercial relations as never before. In the world of fine art the name of Jesus has inspired the finest paintings, the sweetest music, and the grandest architecture.

When Haydn was old, he attended a concert at which his own masterpiece, *The Creation*, was sung. It begins, you know, with a representation of chaos and darkness, by grating sounds and some discordant notes; then "Let there be light" bursts upon the audience in a very cyclone of melody. When this point was reached, the old musician, unable to contain his feelings, arose and pointed upward, as if to say, "That came from God."

So the masters of music, painting, and architecture may point to Christ as the Author of their highest inspirations. Every battle for the liberation of the oppressed, every institution for the education of the orphan, every movement for the protection of the weak against the strong, means that Jesus is still in the world rousing the people to noble endeavor.

The state of mind which leads one to inquire the reason of this, and to investigate the claims of Christ, is a mark of strength. To sit by the highway of time with stolid indifference to such a world movement is not to one's credit. What Christ is doing in the world today should arouse a spirit of inquiry, and make all who are blind to His deity ask questions, and seek to answer them by searching investigation. The result of such inquiry will be the confirmation of His claims.

It Is a Faith That Prays

"Jesus, thou Son of David, have mercy on me." He pleads no merit; he recognizes guilt somewhere. Whether his blindness was a result of sin we know not, but he knew that he was a sinner at heart. The spirit that makes light of sin fosters blindness of soul. The spirit that confesses sin shows true nobility. To acknowledge a fault, and seek to correct it, is an honor; to hide it, that we may foster it, is a shame. "Jesus stood." The cry of the penitent soul stops Him. I can imagine Him paying little attention to a triumphal procession entering the gates of the city with bands of music and rich trophies. He cares little for such gewgaws of earth, but He is as sensitive to the cry of a penitent soul as a mother's heart is to the cry of her child. A broken heart always has the right of way to Jesus. Everything else, however important, is laid aside while He attends to the cry for mercy. Let no penitent sinner feel that the God who has the care of the universe is too busy to look after his case.

It Is a Faith That Fights Its Way to Success

It was a sad fact that the disciples of Jesus sometimes failed to show His spirit of sympathy. They told the blind man to hold his peace, but "he cried so much the more. Thou Son of David, have mercy on me." He would not be silenced; his need was too great. The followers of Jesus should be careful not to hinder rather than help seekers after sight. But indifference may be a quiet rebuke which says, "Hold your peace." A thoughtless criticism of the sermon may have the same effect. These chilling words might have driven away a less courageous soul than Bartimaeus, but his sense of deepest need made him stand his ground and fight his way. Those who would come to Jesus must sometimes press through no little opposition. Where the hand of encouragement should be given the word of rebuke is sometimes spoken. Bartimaeus had assurance that Jesus wanted him, and that was enough to make him brave against all opposers.

> I'll go to Jesus though my sins
> Like a mountain rose,
> I know His courts, I'll enter in,
> Whatever may oppose.

It Is a Faith That Expresses Its Great Need

Jesus said, "What wilt thou that I should do unto thee?" He might have replied, "Give me some money, Lord, that I may be relieved for several days, at least, from begging; give me a home and friends to take care of me." No, no, Bartimaeus was wiser than that. He knew that his deepest need was not money, or clothing, or shelter, but sight. His poverty was the result of his blindness, and if the blindness can be cured, everything else might be remedied. Prayer is need packed until it takes fire. Our deepest needs should be satisfied first. You need an education? Seek it, but not until your soul has been brought into right relations with God. You need money? Make it, but not until you have secured the riches of grace in Christ Jesus. Let not the good hinder the best. "Seek ye first the kingdom of God and his righteousness, and all these things shall be added." May God save us from the illusion that if we seek successfully these things, the kingdom of God shall be added. Let us put first what God has put first. Soul-sight is our deepest need. May we be satisfied with nothing less than the best that Christ can give us.

It Became a Faith That Followed Jesus

He may have had a wife and children in some humble home, and his heart yearned to look into their faces, but Christ who had given him sight was so attractive that he could not leave Him; he must gaze into His loving countenance and use the new eyes he had received in beholding His beauty. I have heard of a man who had lost his sight, and it was restored by an eminent physician. After several days in a dark room, the man's wife and children were brought in, and he looked into their faces for the first time in years, and then he exclaimed, "Oh, where is the man who gave me my sight; his face should have been the first upon which I looked." Thus felt Bartimaeus. Christ was to him all and in all. To be with Him was his delight, to hear His voice his joy, and now forever to do His will his highest ambition.

Such a Faith Glorified Jesus

The word does not mean that he followed along the way shouting "Hallelujah" and singing. It has in it the idea of showing forth the excellence of another. Bartimeus, when he met his old friends, told them of what Jesus had done for him and could not say enough in His praise. I can see him approaching a group on the street corner and pointing to the Master across the way as he says, "There is the Man who gave me my new eyes; let us go and worship Him together." And he was such a man as Christ could afford to take with Him as a sample of His gracious work. The new eyes spoke for themselves. Does our following Christ really glorify Him? Are we such samples of grace that others looking upon us are reminded of our Lord?

NOTES

Now a Certain Man Was Sick

John A. Broadus (1827–1895) has long been recognized as the "Dean of American teachers of homiletics." His work *The Preparation and Delivery of Sermons,* in its many revisions, has been a basic textbook for preachers since it was first published in 1870. Born and educated in Virginia, Broadus pastored the Baptist church at Charlottesville and in 1859 became Professor of New Testament Interpretation and of Homiletics at the Southern Baptist Theological Seminary. He was named president of the school in 1888.

This sermon was preached at the Calvary Baptist Church, New York city, Sunday evening, June 17, 1877.

John A. Broadus

10

NOW A CERTAIN MAN WAS SICK

Now a certain man was sick, named Lazarus, of Bethany, the town of Mary and her sister Martha (John 11:1).

THIS BETHANY IS distant from another town of the same name, beyond Jordan which had just before been alluded to by the apostle as the residence of two Christians who had become well known, Mary and her sister Martha. And to make sure what persons they were, the Evangelist adds, "It was that Mary which anointed the Lord with ointment, and wiped his feet with her hair." The Lord had declared that wherever this gospel was preached throughout the world that story should be told, and here a number of years later, Christians were presumed to be familiar with it. So the evangelist explains it was that Bethany, that Mary. This little town, an insignificant village in itself, has become so well known to all true lovers of the gospel that it would be well to begin the discourse this evening by some little account of the way it appeared a few years ago to the preacher.

You go out of Jerusalem on the east side through a gate they call St. Stephen's gate and immediately begin rapidly to descend a steep bank down into a ravine, down away down you go and across the valley of the Kedron—there is a stream of water there during the rainy season, not at other times—perhaps a hundred yards you go and there you reach the foot of a long hill which we call the Mount of Olives. Just at the foot of it there is a little enclosure of less than an acre, a high wall around it, and some old olive trees—1,000 years old—and that is the place they call Gethsemane. We do certainly know that it was very near there, and you may try to imagine how you would feel if you should go to that spot. I remember one night about the time of Easter, the Passover, a party of us

Americans got a permit and guard from the Turkish authorities to go there, and we knew as we knelt on the earth and prayed that we could not be far away from the spot where Jesus knelt, and fell, and writhed in His agony.

If you wish to climb the Mount of Olives you will see that there are three paths. By the limestone ridges you can see that the paths are where they must have always been. They are long sloping depressions going up three ways. The paths must always have gone up those slight depressions and nowhere else. The northernmost is the path King David went when he fled from Absalom. The southernmost of these was the Roman paved road which to find a better grade passes some degrees to the south. There are pieces of pavement now on the road. There is one bit of pavement just alongside of the ridge of Olivet where Jesus came riding from Bethany in triumphant procession. You can find the very point and you can know that you are within five steps of the very place where Jesus was when He beheld the city and wept over it. There is a shorter path where our Lord and His disciples were wont to go, and if one finds that path he would be apt to seat himself on the rock there and look over the city just as Jesus did when He predicted the destruction of Jerusalem.

When you reach the summit, you are one and a half miles from Bethany, or as we are told in the story, fifteen furlongs. If you go beyond the ridge of Olivet you find an outlying rounded wall which is connected with the ridge of Olivet by a narrow neck of land having deep ravines on the north of it and the south of it, and as you go over that narrow neck of land you know that you cannot be away many paces from where His feet used to tread. Then you pass beyond the outlying wall toward the east and there is a town which has always been called Lazarus' town. You can see the Dead Sea very plainly in the distance from the summit of the Mount of Olives.

And just north of the little town there comes down a ridge or spine of land, and over that comes the same Roman road which has come winding around and then goes over that ridge toward Jericho and the Jordan. Over that little ridge came Jesus, even then, we fancy over that pavement. At one point of the road there is a limestone rock which may have been the spot where Jesus and His disciples sat down to rest when weary. It would be vain to try to describe the feelings with which you sit down here and take out your Bible and read the stories of what went on at Bethany.

The Previous Relations of Jesus to the Family at Bethany

I wish to speak this evening of the raising of Lazarus in particular, but first of all of the previous relations of Jesus to this family at Bethany. These relatives were singularly intimate and familiar. The first time we find the family mentioned is some months before this, the time He said, "One thing is needful." It is evident that He had often been there before. When Martha speaks it is with a certain kind of familiarity.

They were persons of wealth it is evident, and so the large company of men could come as often as they pleased and would not be a burden to them. That they were persons of wealth appears partly from the fact that many Jews had gone out from the city to condole with them in their grief. It shows that they possessed what we call social consideration. Later than this we find that Mary had a valuable quantity of ointment which cost more than three hundred Roman denares—that would be four hundred dollars or five hundred dollars. It would have been out of question if this family had been poor that this woman should have had such a valuable quantity of perfumery, and that explains Mary's course on the previous occasion.

Now on this occasion what Martha did was probably not from a worldly spirit but probably from a desire natural with housekeeping women who in their desire to provide an elegant and elaborate entertainment carry it too far. And so in this case what Martha did was not from a worldly spirit but she went too far in expressing her love for the Prophet of Nazareth. This seems to have led also to a certain familiarity of friendship for we find them often speaking in a kind of fault-finding way to Jesus. Martha comes in to tell the Lord that her sister has left her to do all the work alone, as if He ought to care. And so in our narrative before us we shall find them finding fault with the Master. Do you know I stop there and find myself touched by that. Jesus was not forbidding. Little children loved to come to Him, and He loved to have them come, and His intimate friends would take liberties with Him, and were surprised at His doing some things which they thought were strange.

The Lord's Remarkable Conduct When He Received the News That Lazarus Was Sick

He was away beyond Jordan two or three days journey when the message was brought to Him, and so far as we can see or judge He had no intimation of what would happen. Jesus stayed there two days still. And doubtless when the messenger returned, and Jesus came not, the beloved brother was dead already. They waited there the weary hours of a whole day and another slow moving day, and waiting they wondered that Jesus came not, just as you have wondered many a time, when you have been in trouble and did not need to send a messenger far away beyond a river, just as you have lifted up your heart in prayer to that same Savior now ascended, and wondered that He seemed not to hear. You cried to Him in your agony, and there came neither voice nor sound. There was no sign that He ever heard you at all, or ever would hearken to your cry of distress.

But we know how it was with Martha and Mary. We know that He was preparing a richer, sweeter blessing for them than they had ever dared to dream of or hope for. Now when the disciples remonstrated with Jesus and said to Him, "Master, of late the Jews have sought to stone thee, and goest thou thither again?" our Lord makes a reply which seems a little ambiguous but the general drift is plain. He says: "Are there not twelve hours in the day? If any man walk in the day, he stumbleth not, because he seeth the light of this world." The general thought is, that there is a time to do things, and when the time comes for doing a thing then you need not fear. It had been best that He should come away from Jerusalem to avoid collision with the authorities, but now there was a duty to be performed, and it was right that He should go back again. Ah, when a man can see his plain duty though it be perilous, what a comfort it is.

To my mind, Christian friends, the sorest trials of life come when you cannot make up your mind what is your duty, when you see the time is coming that you will be compelled to decide and you don't know and can't determine what is your duty; but whenever a man can see plainly in his best judgment, and when the best counsel of others does seem the indication of God's providence and clear duty, his duty is not much in this world after all.

Ah, duty will triumph over danger and the heart that is sure of duty can move forward without fear. When Lazarus was dying one of the disciples made a remark— Thomas called Didymus—"Let us also go that we may die with him." This was the man so often spoken of as the type of a skeptic or disbeliever. Thomas appears to be a low-spirited man who took the worst view of things. He will die, he said, let us go and die with him.

Our Lord's Arrival at Bethany and What Followed

Martha may have had somebody looking out for Him, or else must have been very sharply looking out herself, for it was a little town. She met Him before He entered the village. When Martha came where Jesus was she said, "Lord, if thou hadst been here"—the emphasis is not on the "thou." It is not "If *thou* hadst been here," but— "Lord, if thou hadst been *here*," or, Anybody would have supposed that You would have been here, instead of beyond the Jordan, where so dear a friend was ill. "Lord, if thou hadst been here, my brother had not died." But she adds: "But I know that even now whatsoever thou shalt ask of God, God will give it thee."

Do you see what she is thinking of? She is afraid to say it, afraid almost to think it, but the idea is in her mind that He may do something still. I suppose she had heard of like events before. I suppose that many a time when the disciples and the Master were at home, when Martha would have been sitting at Jesus' feet and listening to His profound discourse and they may have told her about the miracles and how when the little girl lay dead, Jesus had lifted her up alive and given her back to her parents, or how when walking along they happened to see a funeral procession and Jesus bade them set down the bier and touched the young man that lay dead and bade him arise, and he stood up and was restored to his mother.

And so she has a thought in her mind which she does not dare distinctly to express. Now then Jesus said to her, "Thy brother shall rise again." Ah, that is ambiguous. She says: "I know that he shall rise again in the last day." Jesus said: "I am the resurrection and the life; he that believeth in me, though he were dead, yet shall he live, and whosoever liveth and believeth in me shall never die." You see He passes as He often does from the idea of physical to spiritual life and death.

Then Martha said: "Yea Lord; I believe that thou art the Christ, the Son of God which should come into the world." Did you ever talk with a Jew, a Jew of the present time to whom the question of all earth's questions was whether Jesus Christ is the Messiah? Perhaps that would help you realize what was meant when she said: "Lord, I believe that thou art the Messiah." "And when she had so said she went her way and called her sister secretly, saying, the Master is come and calleth for thee. As soon as she heard that she arose quickly and came unto him."

Many Jews had come from Jerusalem, ladies and gentlemen, to condole with the family. They were seated in the house condoling after the Oriental fashion. The Oriental fashion is to take a seat there and say nothing—scarcely ever speaking a word. Many a time when I was pastor I remember to have observed, as physicians have observed, how much harm is done by words. Mary sat there with these friends and when Mary was told that the Master had come and called for her she got up and went quickly out of the room. The friends supposed she had gone to the grave to weep there.

When Mary came to where Jesus was she said the same thing that her sister had said, "Lord if thou hadst been here my brother had not died," and then she said no more but fell to weeping. With active and thoughtful Martha, Jesus reasoned; with tender loving Mary, He wept. He always deals with His followers according to their dispositions. Some will serve Him in a cheerful way, others in a half-desponding fashion. Some will serve Him in contemplation more, some in activity. True love of Jesus Christ will show itself as a different thing according to the temperament of the person who exercises it. Let us not set up some standard and refuse to be contented or grateful unless we can be just that, for the standard will often be just what we cannot attain to.

Now as it is rendered, Jesus groaned in spirit. That is not the meaning; the meaning is, "He rebuked Himself," He rebuked Himself when He saw Mary weeping and the friends around also weeping. He agitated Himself; He tried to keep from weeping. When a man feels like weeping, the first thought is that He must restrain Himself, when a woman feels like weeping she will often allow herself to weep without effort. Jesus said, "Where have ye laid him?" And then His feelings gave way, "Jesus wept." My friend, O my friend, it is not any more important for you to realize that He was more than man than it is important for you to realize that He was a man, a tender, loving man, a man with perfect, complete humanity— only, blessed exception, that He was without sin.

And so they went on to the grave. It was a cave we are told. You will find a number of old tombs around Jerusalem now, some only caves and others artificial chambers, some opening into another in which bodies wrapped in clothes were placed and clothes put over them. There is just a little door at the side so that a huge stone rolled over it would protect it from robbers and wild beasts. Jesus said as He came near, "Take ye away the stone." Martha forgets what the Master had said in the feeling that it would not do to take away the stone, and she insinuates to the Lord that it would not do to take away the stone. Jesus rebuked her, "Said I not unto thee, that, if thou wouldest believe, thou should see the glory of God?"

Now my friends you know that story, you used to hear it told when you were a little child, and when you learned to read, that was one of the stories you loved to read. You know how Jesus stood there and said, "Father, I thank thee that thou hast heard me. And I know that thou hearest me always; but because of the people which stand by I said it, that they may believe that thou hast sent me." In loving compassion for these Jews that were out there from Jerusalem, He wanted to say something which could make them believe for their own good. He spoke in a loud voice and said, "Lazarus, come forth." I remember in Bethany one day I almost thought I heard come sounding down from the clouds above that loud voice with which the Redeemer called to the dead man in his tomb to come forth.

And while they held their breath to listen, and their hearts stopped beating to hear, slowly, slowly, out of the tomb, moving with difficulty because wrapped in grave clothes—slowly, slowly came out of the tomb alive, the man, and with a cry of joy Martha rushed to her brother but Mary fell at the Redeemer's feet.

Two or Three Lessons Which This Story Teaches

My friends there are two or three of the many lessons which this marvelous, pathetic story teaches which I will indicate before we turn away. Cherish the miracles, cherish the miracles. We live in a day when many well meaning men, puzzled with the idea of many physical forces, infatuated, will tell you they cannot believe in the possibility of miracles. "I believe there is a Creator, I believe there is a God, but I can't believe in miracles." If God made this universe, with all its physical forces, why can't He who made them control them? Ah, if you believe in a Creator there cannot be any difficulty. When the material world seems closed in around us and men's minds are possessed with materialism so often in this day of ours, cherish the miracles, the Spirit of God who made the material world has in these miracles spoken to us bidding us understand that spirit is mightier than matter; that He is Master of the world He has made and they are the sign manual of the Deity. Stamped upon the mission of His Son, and the teachings of His chosen One, cherish the miracles, and my brother, try to get near Jesus Christ and the Gospel. You may like to go to Palestine; to one who is prepared for it and will stay long enough to profit by it, it is valuable. But it is not necessary to go to Palestine that you may come to Jesus.

These stories carry about them in this world an atmosphere of their own, they carry Jesus with them, and if you will bend over these stories, you will find that you can come nearer Jesus. If you try to see Him and try to hear Him you will find that it becomes possible more and more as you grow older. Many cultivated people think the Gospel is for the Sunday school children, they possibly lose themselves in speculations about prophecy, or turn to precepts or devotions, but there is nothing we need more than to come to the Gospels and try to come there to the Savior, the personal Redeemer, who is the sum of all truth—the way, and the truth, and the life. Try to come near to Jesus in the Gospel, for after all, high or low, refined or rude, young or old, to get near to Jesus, to love Him, and trust Him, and follow Him, and try to do what He wants us to do, to be exceedingly concerned to have others follow Him too, that, that is to be a Christian. In all simplicity of soul, in loving trust and loving obedience try to get near to Jesus in the Gospel and then by the grace of His spirit to follow Him through life.

The Healing of One Born Blind

Charles Haddon Spurgeon (1834–1892) was undoubtedly the most famous minister of the last century. Converted in 1850, he united with the Baptists and soon began to preach in various places. He became pastor of the Baptist church in Waterbeach in 1851, and three years later he was called to the decaying Park Street Church, London. Within a short time the work began to prosper, a new church was built and dedicated in 1861, and Spurgeon became London's most popular preacher. In 1855, he began to publish his sermons weekly; today they make up the fifty-seven volumes of *The Metropolitan Tabernacle Pulpit*. He founded a pastor's college and several orphanages.

This sermon is taken from *The Metropolitan Tabernacle Pulpit*, Volume 18.

Charles Haddon Spurgeon

11

THE HEALING OF ONE BORN BLIND

Since the world began was it not heard that any man opened the eyes of one that was born blind (John 9:32).

THAT WAS QUITE TRUE: there was no instance recorded in Scripture or in profane history at the time when this man spoke of any person who was born blind having obtained his sight. I believe it was in the year 1728 that the celebrated Dr. Cheselden, of St. Thomas' Hospital, for the first time in the world's history achieved the marvel of giving sight to a man who had been blind from his youth up, and since then the operation of couching the eyes has been several times successfully performed upon persons who were born blind.

This man was, however, quite correct in the statement that then, and in his day, neither by skillful surgery nor even by miracle had birth blindness been healed. No doubt this man was a great student in the matter of blindness; it touched so nearly his own consciousness, since he himself dwelt beneath its perpetual shadow. He was the one man in the city who understood the subject thoroughly; but, alas, by all his researches he found no ground for hope. Having learned the whole history of blindness and its cure, this man had come to the assured conviction that none ever had been healed who were in his plight—a mournful conclusion indeed for him.

Our Lord Jesus did for him what never had been done before for any man. This pleasing fact seems to me to be full of consolation to any persons here present who labor under the idea that theirs is a most peculiar and hopeless case. It probably is not so solitary and special a case as you think, but even if we grant your supposition, there is no room for despair since Jesus delights to open up new paths of grace. Our Lord is inventive in love; He devises new modes of mercy. It is His joy to find out and relieve those whose miserable condition has baffled all other help. His mercy is not bound by precedents. He preserves a freshness and originality of love. If you can find no instance in which a person like you has ever been saved you should not, therefore, conclude that you must necessarily be lost; but, rather, you should believe in Him who does great wonders, yes, and marvels unsearchable in the way of grace.

He does as He wills, and His will is love. Have hope that inasmuch as He sees in you a singular sinner, He will make of you a singular trophy of His power to pardon and to bless. It was so with this man's eyes: if never eyes that had been born blind were opened before, Jesus Christ would do it, and the greater would be the glory brought to His name by the miracle. Jesus does not need showing the way, He loves to strike out paths for Himself, and the greater the room for His mercy the better He likes the road.

I purpose this morning gathering instruction from the particular expression which the healed man here used. May the Holy Spirit make the meditation truly profitable to us.

First, I shall ask you to observe *the peculiarity of his case*—he was a man born blind: then, secondly, *the specialties of his cure* shall occupy a little of our attention; and, thirdly, we shall make a few remarks upon *the singular condition of the healed man* from the moment that his eyes were opened.

The Peculiarity of His Case

The peculiarity of his case was not an instance of want of light; that might both speedily and easily have been remedied. There was light enough all around him, but the poor creature had no eyes. Now, there are millions of persons in the world who have little or no light; darkness covers the earth and gross darkness the people. It is the church's business to spread light on all sides, and for this work she is well qualified. We ought not to suffer any person to perish for lack of knowing the Gospel. We cannot give men eyes, but we can give them light. God has placed among us His golden candlesticks and expressly said, "Ye are the light of the world."

Now, I believe that there are some persons who have eyes who, nevertheless, see but little for want of light; they are children of God, but they walk in darkness and see no light; God has given to them the spiritual faculty of sight, but as yet they are down in the mines, in the region of night and deathshade. They are imprisoned in Doubting Castle, where only a few feeble rays struggle into their dungeon. They walk like men in a mist, seeing and yet not seeing. They hear doctrines preached which are not the pure truth, the winnowed corn of the covenant, and, while their eyes are blinded with chaff and dust, they themselves are bewildered and lost in a maze.

Too many in this murky light weave for themselves theories of doubt and fear which increase the gloom; their tears defile the windows of their souls. They are like men who hang up blinds and shutters to keep out the sun. They cannot see, though grace has given them eyes. May it be yours and mine by explanation and example, by teaching with the language of the lips, and the louder language of our lives, to scatter light on all sides, that those who dwell in spiritual midnight may rejoice, because for them light has sprung up.

Again, *this was not the case of a man blinded by accident.* Here, again, the help of man might be of much service. Persons who have been struck with blindness have been again recovered. Notably is this instanced in Bible history when Elijah struck a whole army with blindness, but afterward prayed to God for them and they received their sight at once. There is much that we can do in cases where the blindness is rather to be traceable to circumstances than to nature.

For instance, everywhere in the world there is a degree of blindness caused by prejudice. Men judge the truth before they hear it; they form opinions about the Gospel not having studied the Gospel itself. Put the New Testament into their hands, entreat them to be candid, and to investigate it with their best judgments and to seek guidance from the Holy Spirit, and I believe many would see their error and amend. There are some true spirits whose mental perceptions are blinded by prejudice, who would be helped very graciously to see the truth if we would tenderly and wisely put it before them. The prejudices of education sway many in this country.

We are to the backbone a very conservative people, tenacious of established error, and suspicious of any long-neglected truth. Our countrymen are not soon moved to receive the most obvious truth, unless it has been in vogue for ages. Perhaps it is better that we should be so than that we should be whirled about with every wind of doctrine and should run after every novelty, as some other nations do; but for this cause the Gospel has in this country to combat a mass of prejudice. "Such were my fathers, such ought I to be." "Such our family has always been, therefore such will I be and such shall my children be." No matter how sure may be the truth that is brought before some men's minds, they will not even give it a hearing because old men, good men, and men in authority have decided otherwise. Such persons assume that they are right by inheritance and orthodox by ancestry; they cannot learn anything, they have reached the fullness of wisdom and there they mean to stop.

The church of God should try to remove all prejudices from human eyes from whatever sources they may come. Such opthalmia we may be able to cure; it is within our province to attempt it. Like Ananias, we may remove the scales from the eyes of some blinded Paul. When God has given eyes we may wash the dust out of them. Mingle with your fellowmen, tell them what the faith is that has saved you, let them see the good works which the grace of God produces in you, and as the Gospel at first removed from men's eyes the scales of Judaism, of the Greek philosophy, and of the Roman pride, so doubtless in this land and in this age it will make short work of the prejudices which some are doing their best to foster.

But this was not the case of a man who was blind by accident, and consequently not a type of an understanding darkened by prejudice. *The man was blind from his birth*; his was the blindness of nature, and, therefore, it baffled all surgical skill; concerning the blindness caused by human depravity, the blindness that comes with us at our birth, and continues with us until the grace of God causes us to be born again, I may say, that since the beginning of the world, it has not been heard that any man has opened the eyes of one whose spiritual blindness was born with him and is a part of his nature.

If it be something from without that blinds me, I may recover; but if it be something from within which shuts out the light, who is he that can restore my vision? If from the beginning of my existence I am full of folly, if it be a part if my nature to be without understanding, how dense is my darkness! How hopeless is the fancy that it can ever be removed except by a divine hand! Let us think and say what we will, we are everyone of us by nature born blind to spiritual things: we are not capable of perceiving God, not capable of perceiving the Gospel of His dear Son; not capable of understanding the way of salvation by faith in such a practical way as to be saved by it.

Eyes have we, but we see not; understandings we have, but those understandings are perverted, they are like balances put out of gear, or a compass which forgets the pole. We judge, but we judge unrighteously; by nature we put bitter for sweet, and sweet for bitter; we put darkness for light, and light for darkness; and this is inbred in our nature, wrought into our very constitution; you cannot get it out of man, because it is a part of the man—it is his nature.

If you ask me why it is that man's understanding is so dark, I reply, because his whole nature is disordered by sin: his other faculties having been perverted act upon his understanding and prevent its acting in a proper manner. There is a confederacy of evil within which deceives the judgment and leads it into captivity to evil affections. For instance, our carnal hearts love sin, the set of our unrenewed souls is toward evil. We were conceived in sin and shapen in iniquity, and we as naturally go after evil as the swine seeks out filth.

Sin has a fascination for us, we are taken by it like

birds with a lure, or fishes with a bait. Even those of us who have been renewed have to watch against sin because our nature so readily inclines to it. With much diligence and great labor, we climb the ways of virtue, but the paths of sin are easy to the feet; is not that because our fallen nature inclines in that direction? You have only to relax your energy, and to loose your soul from its anchor-hold, and it drifts at once downward toward iniquity, for so the current of nature runs. It needs much power to send us upward, but downward we go as readily as a stone falls to the ground. You know it is so; man is not as God made him, but his affections are corrupt.

Now, it is certain that the affections very often sway the judgment. The balances are held unfairly, because the heart bribes the head. Even when we fancy that we are very candid we have insensible leanings. Our affections, like Eve, seduce the Adam of our understanding, and the forbidden fruit is judged to be good for food. The smoke of the love of sin blinds our mental eye. Our desire is often father to our conclusion, we think we are judging fairly, but we are really pandering to our baser nature. We think this thing to be better because we like it better; we will not condemn a fault too severely because we have a leaning that way; neither will we commend an excellence, because it might cost our flesh too dear to be able to reach it; or the not reaching it might strike too severe a blow upon our consciences. Ah, while our natural love of sin covers the mind's eye with cataract, and even destroys its optic nerve, we need not wonder that the blindness is beyond removal by any human surgery.

Moreover, our natural pride and self-reliance revolt against the Gospel; we are every one of us very important individuals. Even if we sweep a street crossing we have a dignity of self which must not be insulted. A beggar's rags may cover as much pride as an alderman's gown. Self-importance is not restricted to any one position or grade of life. In the pride of our nature we are all accounted by ourselves to be both great and good, and that which would in any way lower us we repudiate as unreasonable and absurd; we cannot see it, and are angry that others should.

He who makes us suspect our own nothingness teaches a doctrine hard to be understood. Pride will not and cannot understand the doctrines of the Cross because they ring her death knell. In consequence of our natural self-sufficiency we all aspire to enter heaven by efforts and deservings of our own.

We may deny human merit as a doctrine, but flesh and blood everywhere lusts after it; we want to save ourselves by feelings if we cannot by doings, and to this we cling as for dear life. When the Gospel comes with its sharp ax, and says, "Down with this tree! Your grapes are gall, your apples are poison, your very prayers need to be repented of, your tears need to be wept over, your holiest thoughts are unholy, you must be born again, and you must be saved through the merits of another, by the free, undeserved favor of God," then straightway all our manliness, dignity, and excellence stand up in indignation and we resolve never to accept salvation on such terms. That refusal assumes the shape of a want of power to understand the Gospel. We do not and cannot understand the Gospel because our notions of ourselves stand in the way. We start with wrong ideas of self and so the whole business is made confusion and we ourselves are blinded.

Again, beloved, one reason why our understanding does not and cannot see spiritual things is because we judge spiritual things by our senses. Imagine a person who should take a foot rule as his standard of everything which exists in nature, and conceive that this man with his foot rule in his pocket becomes an astronomer. He looks through the telescope and he observes the fixed stars. He is told when he takes out his foot rule that it is quite out of place in connection with the heavens, he must give up his feet and inches, and calculate by millions of miles. He is indignant. He will not be deluded by such enthusiasm. He is a man of common sense, and a foot rule is a thing which he can see and handle; millions of miles are mere matters of faith, no one has ever traveled them, and he does not believe in them. The man effectually closes his own eyes; his understanding cannot develop within such limits.

Thus we measure God's corn with our own bushel; we cannot be brought to believe that "as the heavens are higher than the earth, so are his ways higher than our ways, and his thoughts than our thoughts." If we find it hard to forgive, we dream that it is the same with God. Every spiritual truth is acted upon in the same way. We propose to measure the ocean of divine love in thimblefuls, and the sublime truths of revelation we estimate by drops of the bucket. We shall never be able to reach the thoughts and things of God while we persist in judging after the sight of the eyes, according to the measure of an earthbound, carnal mind.

Our understanding also has become unshipped and out of gear, from the fact that we are at a distance from God, and that consequently we do not believe in Him. If we lived near to God, and habitually recognized that in Him we live and move and have our being, we should accept everything that He spoke as being true, because He spoke it; and our understanding would be clarified at once by its contact with truth and God. But now we think of God as a remote person: we have no love to Him by nature, nor any care about Him. It would be the best news some sinners could hear if there were information given that God was dead; they would rejoice above all things at the thought that there was no God. The fool always says "no God" in his heart, even when he does not dare say it with his tongue. We all by nature would be glad to be rid of God; it is only when the Spirit of God comes and brings us near to God, and gives us faith in our heavenly Father, that we joy and rejoice in Him, and are able to understand His will.

Thus, you see, our entire nature, fallen as it is, operates to the blinding of our eyes, and therefore the opening of the eye of the human understanding toward divine things remains an impossibility to any power short of the divine. I believe there are some brethren whose notion is that you can open a sinner's blind eye by rhetoric. As well hope to sing a stone into sensibility. They dream that you must enchant man with splendid periods, and then the scales will fall from his eyes. The climax is a marvelous engine, and the peroration is more wonderful still; if these will not convince men, what will? To finish a discourse with a blaze of fireworks, will not that enlighten? Alas, we know well enough that sinners have been dazzled a thousand times by all the pyrotechnics of oratory, and yet have remained as spiritually blind as ever they were. A notion has been held by some that you must argue the truth into men's minds, that if you can put the doctrines of the Gospel before them in a clear, logical, demonstrative form they must give way. But, truly, no man's eyes are opened by syllogisms. Reason alone gives no man power to see the light of heaven.

The clearest statements and the most simple expositions are equally in vain without grace. I bear witness that I have tried to make the truth "as plain as a pikestaff," as our proverb is, but my hearers have not seen it for all that. The best declaration of truth will not of itself remove birth blindness and enable men to look to Jesus. Nor do I believe that even the most earnest Gospel appeals, nor the most vehement testimonies to its truth will convince men's understandings. All these things have their place and their use, but they have no power in and of themselves to enlighten the understanding savingly.

I bring my blind friend to this elevated spot and I bid him look upon yonder landscape. "See how the silver river threads its way amid the emerald fields. See how yonder trees make up a shadowy wood; how wisely yonder garden, near at hand, is cultivated to perfection; and how nobly yonder lordly castle rises on yon knoll of matchless beauty." See, he shakes his head; he has no admiration for the scene. I borrow poetical expressions, but still he joins not in my delight. I try plain words and tell him, "There is the garden, and there is the castle, and there is the wood, and there is the river—do you not see them?"

"No," he cannot see one of them, and does not know what they are like. What ails the man? Have not I described the landscape well? Have I been faulty in my explanations? Have I not given him my own testimony that I have walked those glades and sailed along that stream? He shakes his head, my words are lost. His eyes alone are to blame.

Let us come to this conviction about sinners; for, if not, we shall hammer away and do nothing: let us be assured that there is something the matter with the sinner himself which *we* cannot cure, let us do what we will with him, and yet we cannot get him saved unless it be cured. Let us feel this, because it will drive us away from ourselves; it will lead us to our God, it will drive us to the strong for strength, and teach us to seek for power beyond our own; and then it is that God will bless us because then we shall be sure to give all the glory to His name.

But I must leave the case: it is the case of a deep-seated blindness of nature which cannot be touched by human skill.

The Specialties of the Cure

Now we shall dwell a little upon the specialties of the cure, not exactly of this man's cure, but of the cure of many whom we have seen. The first is, *it is usually accomplished by the most simple means*. The man's eyes were opened with a little clay put into them, and then washed out at the pool of Siloam. God blesses very slender things to the conversion of souls. It is very humbling, sometimes, to a preacher who thinks, "Well, I did preach a pretty fair sermon that time," to find God does not care a pin about him or his sermon, and that a stray remark he made in the street, which he hardly thought was of any value whatever, was what God has blessed; that when he thought he succeeded best he had done nothing, and when he thought he had succeeded worst then God blessed him.

Many a soul has had his eyes opened by an instrumentality which never dreamed of being so useful; and, indeed, the whole way of salvation is in itself extremely simple, so as to be well compared to the clay and spittle which the Savior used.

I do not find many souls converted by bodies of divinity. We have received a great many into the church, but never received one who became converted by a profound theological discussion. We very seldom hear of any great number of conversions under very eloquent preachers—very seldom indeed. We appreciate eloquence, and have not a word to say against it by itself, but evidently it has no power spiritually to enlighten the understanding, neither does it please God to use the excellency of words for conversion. When Paul laid aside human wisdom and said he would not use the excellency of speech, he only laid aside what would not have been of much service to him. When David put off Saul's armor, and took the sling and the stones, he slew the giant; and giants are not to be conquered today any more than they were then by champions arrayed in Saul's armor. We must keep to the simple things, to the plain Gospel, plainly preached. The clay and the spittle were not an artistic combination, taste was not charmed by them, or culture gratified, yet by these and a wash in Siloah, eyes were opened—even thus it pleases God by the foolishness of preaching to save them that believe.

But, secondly, *in every case it is a divine work.* In this case it was evidently the Lord Jesus who opened the man's eyes literally, and it is always his work by the Holy Spirit spiritually. He gives a man to know spiritual things and to embrace them by faith. No eye is ever opened to see Jesus except by Jesus. The Spirit of God works all our good things in us. Do not let us get away from this belief on any account. The exigencies of some men's doctrinal systems require them to ascribe some measure of power to the sinner; but we know that he is dead in sin and altogether without strength. Beloved, alter your system of divinity, but do not disavow the truth which is now before us, for it stands confirmed by our own daily experience, as well as revealed in the Word of God. It is the Spirit that quickens and enlightens. Blindness of soul yields only to that voice which of old said, "Let there be light."

Next, *this opening of the eyes is often instantaneous,* and when the eye is opened it frequently sees just as perfectly as if it had always been seeing. I saw a few hours ago what I verily believe was the opening of the eyes of one seeking soul. Two inquiring ones came to me in the vestry; they had been hearing the Gospel here for only a short season, but had been impressed by it. They expressed their regret that they were about to move far away, but they added their gratitude that they had been here at all. I was cheered by their kind thanks, but felt anxious that a more effectual work should be wrought in them, and therefore I asked them, "Have you in very deed believed in the Lord Jesus Christ? Are you saved?" One of them replied, "I have been trying hard to believe." "No," I said, "that will not do. Did you ever tell your father that you tried to believe him?" They admitted that such language would have been an insult. I then set the Gospel very plainly before them in as simple language as I could, but one of them said, "I cannot realize it, I cannot realize that I am saved." Then I went on to say, "God bears testimony to His Son, that whosoever trusts in His Son is saved. Will you make Him a liar now, or will you believe His Word?" While I thus spoke, one of them started as if astonished, and she startled us all as she cried, "Oh, sir, I see it all; I am saved. O do bless Jesus for me, for showing me this and saving me; I see it all." The esteemed sister who had brought me these young friends knelt down with them while with all our hearts we blessed and magnified the Lord.

One of the two sisters, however, could not see the Gospel as the other had done, though I feel sure she will. Did it not seem strange that, both hearing the same words, one should come out into clear light and the other should have to wait in the gloom.

The change which comes over the heart when the understanding grasps the Gospel is often reflected in the face, and shines there like the light of heaven. Such newly enlightened souls often exclaim, "Why sir, it is so plain; how is it I have not seen it before now? I understand all I have read in the Bible now, though I cared not for it before. It has all come in a minute, and now I see what I never perceived before." I simply give one instance because it is one among thousands which one has seen, in which the eyes have opened instantly.

I can only compare the enlightened sinner to a person who has been shut up in a dark prison and has never seen the light, and suddenly his liberator opens a window and the prisoner is staggered and amazed at what he sees when he looks abroad on hill and flood. To the believer, heaven-given sight is so superlative a gift, and what is revealed to him so amazes him, that he scarce knows where he is. Very frequently, when Christ opens the eyes it is done in a moment and done completely in that moment, though in other instances it is a more gradual light; men are at first seen as trees walking, and then by degrees film after film is taken from the spiritual eye.

Now, you must not wonder if light comes so suddenly that is should be quite *a new sensation to the man*, and therefore should surprise him. Do you remember the first breath of spiritual life you ever drew? I think I recollect it still. Do you remember the first you ever had of Christ? Oh, you must recollect it. There is fixed in the memories of some of us the first time we saw the sea, and the first time we gazed upon the Alps, but these were nothing; we felt they were still but pieces of this old world, and we had only seen a little more of what we had seen before: but conversion opens up a new world: it teaches us to peer into the invisible and to see the things not seen of mortal eye. When we receive new eyes, we see a thousand things which utterly astound and at the same time delight us.

Do you wonder if young converts get excited? I neither wonder nor blame, I wish we had a little more excitement in our gatherings for worship. Who hears nowadays the cry, "What must I do to be saved?" or who hears a soul saying, "I have found Him of whom Moses in the law and the prophets did write"? Let us give plenty of liberty to the work of the Spirit of God, and believe that when He comes men will not always act after the sober rules of decorum, but will break through them, and even be suspected of being drunken, because they speak as men in their ordinary minds are not likely to do. It is a strange and marvelous thing to men when the Spirit of God opens their eyes, and we must not wonder if they scarce know what they say and forget where they are.

One thing is certain, that when the eye is open, *it is a very clear thing to the man himself.* Others may doubt whether his eyes are opened, but he knows they are; about that he has no question. "One thing I know, whereas I was blind, now I see." When the Lord in His infinite mercy visits a spirit that has been long shut up in the dark, the change becomes so great, that he does not need to inquire, "Am I changed or not?" but he himself is assured of it by his own consciousness.

Once give the man the eye to see, and he possesses a faculty that is *capable of abundant use.* The man who could see the Pharisees, could by and by see Jesus. He who has his eyes opened cannot only see the trees and fields around him, but he can behold the heavens, and the glorious sun: and once give a man spiritual light, he has at once capacity for seeing divine mysteries; he shall see the world to come, and the glories yet to be revealed. Those new-created eyes are those which shall see the King in His beauty, and the land that is very far off; He has the faculty for seeing everything which shall be beheld in the day of the revelation of our God and Savior Jesus Christ.

Oh, what a marvelous work is this! May everyone of us know it personally. I put the question, Do we know it? Have we thus had our eyes opened?

The Condition of the Healed Man

When his eyes were opened first, *he had strong impressions in favor of the glorious One who had healed him.* He did not know who He was, but he knew He must be something very good; he thought He must be a prophet, and when he came to know Him better he felt that He was God, and he fell down and worshiped Him. No man has had his eyes opened without feeling intense love to Jesus, aye, and I will add, without believing in His deity, without worshiping Him as the Son of God.

We do not want to be uncharitable, but we have a little common sense left. We never can see how a man can be a Christian who does not believe in Christ, or how a man can be said to believe in Christ who only believes in the smallest part of Him—receives His humanity, but rejects His Godhead. There must be a real faith in the Son of God, and he is blind and dark still who does not fall down like the man in this story and worship the living God, beholding the glory of God in the face of Jesus Christ, and blessing God that he has found both a Prince and a Savior in the person of the Lord Jesus, who has laid down His life for His people.

Oh, I am sure if your eyes are opened, you love Jesus this morning, you feel your heart leap at the very thought of Him, your whole soul goes after Him, you feel if He has opened your eyes those eyes belong to Him and your whole self too.

This man, therefore, *became from that moment a confessor of Christ.* They questioned him, and he did not speak bashfully, and conceal his convictions, but he answered the questions at once. Stephen was the first martyr, but this man was the first confessor assuredly, and before the Pharisees he put it out plainly and plumply, straight to their faces, in simple language.

And so, beloved, if the Lord has opened our eyes we shall not hesitate to say so. He has done it, blessed be His name! Our tongues might well be smitten with eternal silence if we were to hesitate to declare what Jesus has done for us. I charge you who have received grace from Christ Jesus to become confessors of the faith, to acknowledge Christ as you ought to do. Be baptized and united with His people, and then in whatever company you are, however others may speak for Him or against Him, take your stand and say, "He hath opened mine eyes, and I bless His name."

Now this man *becomes an advocate* for Christ as well as a confessor, and an able advocate too, for the facts, which were his arguments, baffled his adversaries. They said this and that, but he replied, "Whether it be so or no it is not for me to say, but God has heard this man, therefore this man is not a sinner as you say He is; He has opened my eyes, therefore I know where He must have come from, He must have come from God."

We have been arguing for a long time against infidelity, with arguments which have never achieved anything. I believe that skeptics glean their blunted shafts and shoot them at the shield of truth again; I fear that the Christian pulpit has been the great instructor in infidelity, for we have taught our people arguments which they never would have known if we had not repeated them under the notion of replying to them. But, beloved, you will never meet infidelity except with facts.

Say what it is God has done for you, and prove it by your godly lives. Against the holy lives of Christians unbelief has no power. Stand in close ranks, each man with his sword of holy living, panoplied in the power of the Holy Spirit, and the assaults of your foes, however desperate their malice, will utterly fail. God grant us, like this man, to learn the art of arguing for Christ by personal testimony.

Well, then, it came to pass, that this man with his eyes opened was *driven out of the synagogue.* Speckled birds are always hunted away by their fellow birds. One of the worst things that can happen to a man as far as this world is concerned is to know too much. If you will barely keep abreast with the times you may be tolerated, but if you get a little ahead of the age you must expect ill-treatment.

"Be blind among blind men." It is the very dictate of prudence if you would save your skin. It is a very unsafe thing to have your eyes opened among blind men, for they will not believe in your assertions, and you will be very dogmatical, and, as they cannot see, you have no common ground for argument, and you will fall at once to quarreling; and if the blind men shall be in the majority, the probabilities are you will have to go out of door or window, and make yourself company elsewhere.

When God opens a man's eyes to see spiritual things, straightway others say, "What is this fellow talking about? We do not see what he sees." And if the fellow is very simple he turns around to these blind men, and says, "I will explain to you now." Dear friend, you will lose your pains, for they cannot see. If a man is born blind, you need not talk to him about scarlet and mauve and magenta, he cannot understand you, he does not know anything at all about it. Go on, for it is no use reasoning with him; the only thing you can do with him is to take him where he can get his eyes opened. To argue with him is utterly useless, he has not the faculty.

If you knew a person to be devoid of taste you would not quarrel with him because he said sugar tasted like salt; he neither knows what *sweet* means nor what *salt* means, but only uses words without understanding them.

And a man who is without grace in his heart does not and cannot know anything about religion. He catches up the phrases, but he knows as much about the truth itself as a botanist knows about botany who has never seen a flower, or as a deaf man knows of music. Do not try to reason with such people, believe that they are incapable of learning from you by reasoning, and go to God's Holy Spirit, with this cry, "Lord, open their eyes! Lord, open their eyes!

Be very patient with them, for you cannot expect blind men to see, and must not be very angry with them if they do not. But be very prayerful for them, and bring the Gospel to them in the power of the Holy Spirit, and then who knows but their eyes may be opened.

But wonder not if they say you are a "fanatic," an "enthusiast," a "Methodist," "Presbyterian," "cant," "hypocrite"—those are the kind of words which the spiritually blind fling at those who can see. You say you have a faculty which they have not; they, therefore, deny the faculty because they would not like to admit that you have the start of them, and they put you out of the synagogue.

But notice, when this man was put out Jesus Christ found him. It was a blessed loss for him, then, to lose the Pharisees and find his Savior. O brethren, what a mercy it is when the world does cast us out!

I remember an estimable woman of title, who is now in heaven, who, when she was united to this church was forsaken by all those persons of rank who had formerly associated with her; and I said to her, and she joined in the sentiment, "What a mercy you are rid of them. They might have been a snare to you. Now (I said) you will have no further trouble from them." "Yes," and she added, "For Christ's sake I could be content to be accounted as the off-scouring of all things."

The society of the world never was any benefit to us, and it never will be, and trying to be very respectable and to mingle in elevated society, and all that, is a snare to many Christians. Prize men for their real worth and not for their gilt, and believe those to be the greatest men who are the holiest men, and those to be the best company who keep company with Christ.

It is a great blessing to the church when it is persecuted. For the matter of that we might be glad to have back the days of Diocletian again. The church is never purer, on the whole, never more devout, and never increases more rapidly than when she enjoys the bad opinion of society; but when we begin to be thought very excellent people, and our church is honored and esteemed, and respected, corruption sets in, we get away from Christ and prove again that the friendship of this world is enmity with God. The Lord grant that we may have our eyes so opened that our testimony may bring upon us the charge of singularity, and, then, if put away from the company of those who cannot see the Lord, may we live all the closer to Him, and this shall be a great gain to us.

The Lord bless you, beloved, for Jesus Christ's sake. Amen.

NOTES

The Sick of the Palsy

Joseph Parker (1830–1902) was one of England's most popular preachers. Largely self-educated, Parker had pulpit gifts that soon moved him into leadership among the Congregationalists. He was a fearless and imaginative preacher who attracted both common people and the aristocracy, and he was particularly a "man's preacher." His *People's Bible* is a collection of the shorthand reports of the sermons and prayers Parker delivered as he preached through the entire Bible in seven years (1884–91). He pastored the Poultry Church, London, later called the City Temple, from 1869 until his death.

This sermon is taken from *The People's Bible*, Volume 18 (London: Hazell, Watson and Viney, 1900).

Joseph Parker

12

THE SICK OF THE PALSY

And, behold, they brought to him a man sick of the palsy, lying on a bed (Matthew 9:2).

AND HE ENTERED into a ship and passed over and came into his own city." That does not tell us half the truth. A reference to this verse will show you the necessity of reading the Scriptures through, and of paying attention not to the text only, but to the context. Anybody would think, from reading this first verse, that Jesus had, upon His own will and motion, returned into His own city: we should have no hesitation in coming to the conclusion that Jesus did this because He wanted to do it or had willed so to do. Is there not a cause? Refer to the verse which concludes the previous chapter if you would find the key of the verse which opens the ninth chapter. "Behold the whole city came out to meet Jesus, and when they saw him they besought him that he would depart out of their coasts, and he entered into a ship and passed over." Now the whole case is before you. You thought He came away spontaneously, whereas the fact is He was driven out. He never leaves the human heart of His own will; He never said to any one of you, "I have been here long enough, I must now leave you to yourself."

But you tell me that Jesus Christ is no longer with you, you say you sigh to think of happier days, you recall the hour when Jesus Christ was the only guest of your heart, and now you mourn that He is no longer present in the sanctuary of your consciousness and your love. He never left of His own accord. I cannot allow your mourning to go without one or two sharp and piercing inquiries. How did you treat Him—did His presence become a shadow in the life—was His interference burdensome—did He dash some cups of pleasure from your hands—did He call you to

151

sacrifices which were too painful for your love? Search
yourselves and see. I never knew Him to leave a human
heart because He was tired of it, weary because He had
expended His love upon it—but I have known Him
whipped out, scourged away, entreated to go, banished.

"And he entered into a ship and passed over and came
into his own city." How He looked as He did so! No picture can ever tell us how the eyes fell upon the dust in
shame for those who had desired His banishment. How
His heart quivered under a new and sharp pain as He
realized that He was indeed despised and rejected of men!
How He felt as His good deeds became the occasion of a
desire on the part of those who had seen them to send
Him away from their coasts! This is a mystery on which
there is no light. Do not imagine that you began the story
with the first verse of the ninth chapter. It is true that
Jesus entered into a ship and passed over, but it is also
true that the people besought Him that He would depart
out of their coasts. So when my heart is empty of His
presence and I wonder whither He has gone, I will revive
my recollection, I will command my memory to be faithful
and to tell me the white truth, the candid fact, and when
it speaks it will shame me with the intolerable reminis-
cence that I *besought* Him to go. Let us be honest, or we
shall never be healed; let us face the stern, fierce facts of
life, or we shall make no progress in purity or in spiritual
knowledge.

"And behold they brought unto him a man sick of the
palsy, lying on a bed, and Jesus, seeing their faith." Is it
possible for *faith* to be greater than the *palsy?* Are such
miracles wrought in the consciousness of man? Does the
soul ever rise in its original majesty and put the body
down? Sometimes. Is it possible for the will to be so in-
flamed and inspired to rise above the palsy and to say, "I
am master!" I like such flashes of the divinity that is
within us. We are too easily cowed; our physicians com-
plain that our will does not cooperate with their endeavors, so that we too easily go down. There is something in
us that can conquer the palsy. I cannot gather together
all the subtle influences which make up the present

economy of things, but again and again in the history of others, and now and then in my own history, I have seen such a rising up of the inner nature as has said to the body, "I am master." I magnify these occasional revelations of the latent force of a kind of suppressed divinity, until I see death dead, the grave filled up, and the whole universe full of life.

Magnify all the *best* hints of your nature; be ready to accept suggestions of new power; never take the little and dwindling view of your life. If now and then your heart leap up like sparks of fire in prayer seize every one of them. *That* is where your grandeur is; that is your true self. Caught in some mean conception, conscious of some unworthy fancy—know that that is the *leper* that has to be healed. Caught in some rapture of worship, some sweet desire for heaven—know that that is the *angel* that is in you, and that by and by nothing shall be left in you but the angel, the true spirit, conqueror through Him who wrought its redemption.

"And Jesus, seeing their faith—." That was just like Him. He always sees the best of us; He never takes other than the greatest view of our lives and their endeavors. "And Jesus, seeing their faith." Shall we amend the text? "And Jesus, seeing their—sectarianism." That would fill up a line better than *faith*; it is a longer word; it has more syllables in it; it fills the mouth better— shall we put it in? "And Jesus, seeing their—denominationalism." There is a word that would almost make a line by itself. That word ought to have something in it; polysyllables ought not to be empty. "And Jesus, seeing their—congregationalism, their attachment to Episcopalianism, their deep love of Roman Catholicism." I fancy we cannot amend the text. We can take out the little word *faith* and put in the long words I have named; these would not be amendments, they would be spoliations; they would be blasphemies; they would belittle the occasion; they would taint it with a human touch. Let the word *faith* stand; it is universal; it is a cord that stretches itself around the starlit horizon; it touches those of you who belong to no sect, the dumb, the groping, the wondering, as well as the clearminded and the positive as to religious principle and conviction.

Jesus Christ always startled His hearers by seeing something *greater* in them than they had ever seen in themselves, and always seemed to credit His patients with their own cure. He said, "Daughter, thy faith hath made thee whole." He gave the woman to feel as if she had all the time been her own healer. And the broad and everlasting meaning of that assurance is that you and I have it in us at this moment to get the healing that we need. The Physician is here; His prescription is written in syllables clear as stars, and in lines open as the heavens. What He waits for is our faith. "Lord, I believe; help thou mine unbelief." "Lord, increase our faith." "Believe on the Lord Jesus Christ and thou shalt be saved." "Be it unto thee according to thy faith." "Believest thou that I am able to do this?" There is something then for *us* to do. Find it out and do it, and God will be faithful to His Word.

"And Jesus, seeing their faith, said unto the sick of the palsy, Son, be of good cheer, thy sins be forgiven thee." But this was a question of the *palsy*. the man had not come as a *religious* inquirer, had he? I was not aware that Jesus was sitting down somewhere for the purpose of holding religious conversation with people. This man is sick of the palsy; he cannot move a limb; it requires four people to carry him; and Jesus Christ gives a *religious* turn to the event. We want this sick man healed; we do not want to hear anything about *sins*; we are not religious inquirers, we are afflicted men. How we do belittle everything we touch! If we pluck a flower it dies. Jesus Christ said, "All these afflictions have a common root: sin is the explanation of every scab on that leper's brow; and look at the trembling in that paralytic; sin drove the sight from those eyes, and the hearing from those ears, and the strength from those ankle bones. This is the accursed work of sin." He is a fundamental Teacher; He does not treat symptoms; He treats the central and vital *cause* which expresses itself in symptoms so patent and so distressing.

This is the great lesson which the world is so unwilling

to receive. Give us acts of Parliament, give us better houses for this class and for that class, give us better drainage and larger gardens and better ventilation, and we shall cobble the world up to stand on its rickety legs ten years longer. All these things are in themselves right enough; no sane man has one word to speak against them. If they be brought in, however, as *causative*, they must be rejected, they are collateral, they are cooperative, they are helpful, and in that sense they are necessary, but the world's stream will never be pure until the world's fountain has been cleansed. We think we can cure the world by officialism and by small sanitary pedantries, by congresses and conferences—all these things have their place and their use, but until we get at the root and core and center and heart we are as men who are throwing buckets into empty wells and drawing them up again. The world will not believe this, so the world has not yet risen and taken up its bed and walked.

"And, behold, certain of the scribes said within themselves, This man blasphemeth." There again is the belittling which man does in all his interpretations. Oh, if the sermon could be equal to the text in all cases, what preaching we should have and what hearing! Christ said, "Thy sins are forgiven thee." The scribes said, "This man blasphemeth." We always drag down what we touch; the day of rapture is gone, the sacred hour of enthusiasm has withdrawn itself because we have besought it to depart. Men never speak in fire now: we have fallen upon an age of prudence, and word measurement, and we are tricksters in the uses of syllables and in the adaptations of phrases, and never get beyond the poor range of little speech, or utter as with the heart those sentences which are revelations. We like to hear the little mincing voice that dare not utter one word louder than another; we like to hear the multiplication table repeated every Sunday from the first line to the last; we like to keep within statistical proofs and references that have been scheduled and that can be verified. The great prophet of fire, Elijah, is gone—were he to come again we would take him by the throat and thrust him into the dungeon.

The scribes were right from their own point of view. It would have been blasphemy in any one of *them* to have spoken a noble word about anybody. There are some throats that were never made to emit one noble sound. There are men to whom prayers are lies, and revelations are delusions, and prophecies are but the witnesses of the weakness of their speakers. A man cannot hear above his own level. "He that hath ears to hear let him hear." Every *dog* has ears—yes, but not to *hear*. Men carry the standard of judgment within them; from the little man the little judgment, from the great man the noble criticism, from the divinest, the divinest love. It is better to fall into the hands of God than into the hands of men.

"And Jesus, knowing their thoughts—." See how He never relinquishes the *spiritual* line in all this incident. Jesus seeing their faith—that was a spiritual perception: Jesus seeing their thoughts—there is the same power of working mental miracles. He reads our minds; there is no curtain made yet by human hands, how cunning soever, that can shut out those eyes. He understands every pulsation of the heart, He reads every motion of the will, all things are naked and open to the eyes of Him with whom we have to do. The eyes of the Lord run to and fro throughout the whole earth—sometimes the universe seems to me to be all eyes; I am surrounded by eyes of fire. All speech seems to sum itself into one pregnant sentence— "Thou God seest me."

Do not lightly pass over these words, for they open the great sphere of the *mental miracles* performed by Jesus Christ. We are accustomed to read about His physical miracles and to doubt them. Any scribe can doubt. It is no great thing to doubt. The doubter never did anything for the world; the doubter never put one stone upon another. The world is indebted to its faith for its life and for its progress. Jesus not only cured the palsy, He read *thoughts*: already He begins to forecast the day when physical miracles shall depart, and the miracles that shall astound shall be heart-readings, and heart-companionships and spiritual revelations, and moral opportunities and destinies. We live in that dispensation now;

miracles of an ordinary and outward kind have all gone, but the miracles of the Holy Spirit are being performed every day.

"For whether is easier—." It would appear—for I regard this statement as elliptical—that some thought had occurred to the mind of the scribes that it was easy enough to say, "Thy *sins* be forgiven thee," but the thing to do was to cure the man of the *palsy*. It was easy to talk blasphemies, but what about performing the *cure?* There was a kind of self-gratulation as they suggested that Jesus Christ had taken the easy course of talking blasphemies and letting the substantial thing that was to be done alone, so He says, "Whether is easier to say, 'Thy sins be forgiven thee,' or to say 'Rise and walk'?" The scribes committed the mistake which the whole world has ever since been repeating. Where is there a man who does not think of every intellectual effort as quite easy? It is very difficult for a man to walk upon a tight rope across a river—that is something amazing—worth a shilling to look at. But for any man to preach—why, of course that is easy enough, any fool can do that; everybody knows that anybody can preach a sermon! To suggest a *thought*, to flash an idea upon the intellectual horizon—any man in a family who is good for nothing else can do that.

We always send the imbeciles into the church. To go into the army requires a man, and to go into the navy requires a kind of man and a half, and to go into the law requires a good many men, but to go into the church—why, the soft sap of a family will go into the church. This is possible—possible in relation to all the communions into which the great Christian church is broken up. There are no doubt soft men and imbecile men in every pulpit in Christendom—that is to say in every section of the church in Christendom—but do not understand that the intellectual is always so easy. It is sometimes hard work, even to preach. There are those who think the spiritual worthless. It is easy to give advice; nothing could be easier than to address oneself to spiritual necessities, and such service is worthless. Whoever thinks of paying a schoolmaster or a preacher?

There are those who think of religion as merely

sentimental, as having no practical value in it; yet there is not a man among us who does not owe his social status to religion. You would never have had the customers that flock around your counter but for religion; you would never have got your debts collected but for religion; you would never have been saved from the gutter and the workhouse if an angel of religion had not come after you and brought you in. Religion is not a colored cloud, an evaporating sentiment, it is a most practical factor in the creation and redemption and sanctification of human life.

"And when the multitude saw it, they marveled and glorified God." Trust to the great broad human instincts, and do not ask the scribes what they think. Take your case to the scribes and say, "Gentlemen, what is your learned opinion about this man's cure?" and they, having rolled themselves around and around in the thickest bandages of the reddest tape, begin to consider. I have faith in broad human instincts: I will not altogether withdraw from our proverbial sayings— *Vox populi vox Dei*—I know the crowd has been wrong, I know the mob has been out of the way again and again (I am not speaking of mere crowds or mere mobs: I am speaking of the average human instinct all over our civilization), yet it answers the true voice in the long run, it knows the right man, it knows the right cures, it knows the right books. That human instinct is the next best thing for our guidance to divine inspiration. Make friends of the people, and let little cliques and coteries rot in their own isolation.

Observe the course which Jesus Christ takes, "But that ye may know that the Son of man hath power on earth to forgive sins. Arise, take up thy bed and go unto thine house." We must sometimes prove our religion by our *philanthropy.* Sometimes a man can understand a loaf when he cannot master an argument; sometimes a man can understand a kind action done to his physical necessities when he cannot comprehend or apply the utility of a spiritual suggestion; you do not relinquish the ground that the spiritual is higher than the material when you accommodate yourself to the man's weakness and say to him in effect, "You cannot understand this spiritual argument, therefore I will come down to your ground and do what you can understand." Thus the church must often prove its religion by its philanthropy. The world cannot understand our creed, but the world can understand our collection. There are masses of men in London today who could really not understand what I am endeavoring to expound; it is beneath them, or above them, or beyond them, but they will be perfectly able to ascertain what we have done for cases of necessity that may now be appealing to our liberality.

This is God's method of proving His own kingdom and claim. "The goodness of God," the apostle says, "should lead us to repentance." Every good gift given to the body and given to society is an angel that should lead us in a religious direction. God says to us every day, "That ye may know how to care for your souls, I will show you how to care for your bodies." Now what has He done for the body? Look at that lamp He has lighted, now shining as the southern zenith; look at the meadows He has spread and the gardens He has drawn around our habitations; look at the loving air, the hospitable summer, the abundant autumn, the restful sleep of the winter—and if He has done so much for the body, He says, "But that ye may know what I would do for your mind, for your soul, for your higher faculties, I give you these witnesses, that you can lay your hand upon and examine for yourselves."

It is an argument I cannot refute, it is an appeal I would gladly obey.

KREGEL CLASSIC SERMONS Series

Classic Sermons on the Apostle Peter

Classic Sermons on the Attributes of God

Classic Sermons on the Birth of Christ

Classic Sermons on Christian Service

Classic Sermons on the Cross of Christ

Classic Sermons on Faith and Doubt

Classic Sermons on Family and Home

Classic Sermons on Heaven and Hell

Classic Sermons on Hope

Classic Sermons on the Miracles of Jesus

Classic Sermons on the Names of God

Classic Sermons on Overcoming Fear

Classic Sermons on Praise

Classic Sermons on Prayer

Classic Sermons on the Prodigal Son

Classic Sermons on the Resurrection of Christ

Classic Sermons on the Second Coming and
Other Prophetic Themes

Classic Sermons on the Sovereignty of God

Classic Sermons on Spiritual Warfare

Classic Sermons on Suffering

Classic Sermons on Worship